BRAIN FOOD

'Poetic Wisdom for Life'

MEKO

Copyright © 2020 Meko
All rights reserved.

ISBN 13: 978-0-692-14191-5
LCCN: 2019903602
Eagle Life Publications, Dallas, Texas

BRAIN FOOD

POETIC WISDOM

FOR LIFE

Contents

Introduction

Poem 1:	*Fear*	1
Poem 2:	*Happy Go Lucky*	3
Poem 3:	*Encourage Yourself*	5
Poem 4:	*Lover's vs Friends*	7
Poems 5:	*Blessings and More*	9
Poems 6:	*Satellite Vision*	11
Poem 7:	*Your Will Be Done*	13
Poem 8:	*Purest Air Moments*	15
Poem 9:	*Show Me*	17
Poem 10:	*Addiction Free*	19
Poem 11:	*Narcissistic Personality*	21
Poem 12:	*Break the Chains*	23
Poem 13:	*Power Through*	25
Poem 14:	*Wake Up and Be Great*	27
Poem 15:	*Love Flow*	29
Poem 16:	*Illusion Lips*	31
Poem 17:	*Think Tank*	33
Poem 18:	*Spiritual Connection*	35
Poem 19:	*Skin Color*	37
Poem 20:	*Evolve*	39
Poem 21:	*My Muse*	41
Poem 22:	*A Mother's Love*	43
Poem 23:	*Don't Wait*	45
Poem 24:	*Why Wait: Funds Allowed.*	47
Poem 25:	*Machine Being*	49
Poem 26:	*Early Morning Pursuit*	51
Poem 27:	*Amplify Me*	53

Poem 28:	*Loneliness*	55
Poem 29:	*You, Me, Us, We*	57
Poem 30:	*Love Reruns*	59
Poem 31:	*Love Connection*	61
Poem 32:	*Think It, Feel It, Believe It*	63
Poem 33:	*You and I Together*	65
Poem 34:	*Now I See*	67
Poem 35:	*Royal Reigns*	69
Poem 36:	*Music Therapy*	71
Poem 37:	*No Fool's Allowed*	73
Poem 38:	*Connecting with Him*	75
Poem 39:	*Love Thoughts*	77
Poem 40:	*I Feel It Coming*	79
Poem 41:	*Don't Stop*	81
Poem 42:	*Voting Rights*	83
Poem 43:	*Drunken End*	85
Poem 44:	*Good Deeds*	87
Poem 45:	*Physical You*	89
Poem 46:	*Mental Responsibilities*	91
Poem 47:	*Dream Catcher*	93
Poem 48:	*Prosperity*	95
Poem 49:	*Forgive and Makeup*	97
Poem 50:	*When Turning A New Leaf*	99
Poem 51:	*I Am*	101
Poem 52:	*Support System*	103
Poem 53:	*Addicted to Comfort*	105
Poem 54:	*Parent Person*	107
Poem 55:	*Old-Fashioned*	109
Poem 56:	*What's Your Pleasure?*	111
Poem 57:	*Two as One*	113
Poem 58:	*Food Bank*	115
Poem 59:	*Shadow*	117
Poem 60:	*Light Fear*	119
Poem 61:	*Be Patient Love*	121
Poem 62:	*Formal You Formal Me*	123
Poem 63:	*Moving Upstream*	125
Poem 64:	*Close Enemies*	127

Poem 65:	*Reach Out*	129
Poem 66:	*DNA*	131
Poem 67:	*Who Are You?*	133
Poem 68:	*We're Better Now*	135
Poem 69:	*Today's Date*	137
Poem 70:	*Love Mate*	139
Poem 71:	*Views*	141
Poem 72:	*Education in Us*	143
Poem 73:	*Lost Angel*	145
Poem 74:	*Create Your Way*	147
Poem 75:	*Eye Contact*	149
Poem 76:	*Spreading Love*	151
Poem 77:	*Capable Flower*	153
Poem 78:	*Sweetness*	155
Poem 79:	*Women and Men*	157
Poem 80:	*Autism and being Unique*	159
Poem 81:	*Dance with Me*	161
Poem 82:	*100 Percent*	163
Poem 83:	*Score*	165
Poem 84:	*The End*	167
	Afterword	171
	About the Author	173

This *Brain Food* is intended to motivate, inspire, and encourage you to write down a few things about yourself.

Sometimes writing things down has a way of helping us to see ourselves in a real sense of, *How Am I Really?*

Some of us crave to live a certain way, but there is no way around not having to change how we act, eat, think, and react to gaining that real change.

We are all born into this world for a purpose, and it's up to you to decide what will be your legacy. — What is your purpose in this world today?

This Brain Food is food provided to aid intelligence, memory, and creativity for staying on top of your mental health.

Our brain is an extremely metabolically active organ, and that makes it very hungry, and a picky eater at that!

Our brain controls almost everything we do, and when it isn't properly fed. We know what happens; it starves.

But this book is designed to provide a more psychological nutritional view of how we think as prosperous human beings today, with or without proper food intake.

This is food for thought, followed by your input. So let's seek knowledge and empower each other with how to live in this world today.

Grab a pen or pencil for your input.

A divine influence directly and immediately exerted upon the mind or soul should be one of your own.

Encouraging you to marvel at your own lives by sharing thoughts in forms of poems is a fun way of stimulating you to do what you must do!

THAT BUSINESS? START IT.
THAT APP? DEVELOP IT.
THAT BOOK? WRITE IT.
THAT PODCAST? LAUNCH IT.
THAT IDEA? FLESH IT OUT.
THAT GIFT? PUT IT TO USE.

BUT, WE CAN'T USE PRAYER TO REPLACE LAZINESS.

WE MUST PRAY AND DO THE WORK.

Correct Bad Patterns.

Patterns: A combination of qualities, acts, tendencies, and etcetera; forming a consistent or characteristic arrangement. Such as, the behavior *patterns* of doing the same things will typically get you the same results.

Be lifted by these words as you move forward with sharing your thoughts and inspirations.

There is power in accepting your own thoughts and recognizing what you really want, your own truths.

USE YOUR POWER.

Fear

Impending thoughts of distress— we all have this emotion aroused when we feel there's a threat.

Whether real or imagined— being afraid is just another part of life— the strife is when we let it over come us— subdue us, become still and stifled.

Smothered in the mind— but we should choose now to suppress the what if's— release the fear suffocated by the atmosphere. Free yourself and live.

Embrace your fear— accept it— deal with it— face it immediately then abolish it.

There's no shortcuts, no way around it, even when you cry— take a deep breath and allow it to happen. Because these experiences will help you to prevail and take on what you need to handle.

Dwell in the goodness of life and do what's right— our fears are just like important business deals— face it boldly— bravely and with confidence. You'll get what you need.

Pray and be poised— be aware— confront your fears but don't hang on to it. Fear is just an illusion, although it can also be very real.

Fear is OK, it's OK to be afraid. The problems arise when you let it dominate you. — Be brave and face your fears, understand to increase your wisdom you must control or eliminate fear, know when and how to handle your fears.

How do you currently overcome fear? Explain your strengths of how you dominate it!

Even if you haven't quite figured it all out yet, what are your plans for getting past your fears in the future?

It's a distressing emotion aroused by impending danger, evil, pain, etc. What is your security from this? How do you keep calm? Where does your courage come from?

Use the space on the next page to explain your thoughts regarding fear.

'Poetic Wisdom for Life'

Happy Go Lucky

Today is a day that I don't feel so good— but I'm wearing a smile because it's my fate, you are what you feel you are so I'll still strive to be great.

Through sickness and in good health— I live life as though it's all about growth— through good times and bad, I try to find a way not to be tedious or sad.

It only works out when you believe that the bad things will pass— happy go lucky is how you should choose to live even when you're mad.

Sometimes it's hard because pain can change you— you can't help but to be sad— and that's okay too. We all have a right to feel that way, including when we get mad and don't know what to do.

Happy times are ahead— is what to think when you're mad— don't always give in to your sad struggles, push through and fight back instead.

Be happy because you deserve that— as a matter of fact— stop what you're doing right now and hug yourself. You're wonderful, and I know that you can feel that.

The time to be happy is now— spread joy and open-up— because you'll get what you need as the love you put out here will return to you bigger than you've ever seen.

Practice peace, patience, and be proud of your presence— you are what this world needs— positivity— as you pace yourself and succeed.

What is being demonstrated around you? In other words, describe what's manifesting around you. What do you see daily?
Good or bad, what's being established in your world today?

Do you like what you see? If so, great!
If not, what would you change and how will you change it?

Use the space on the next page to explain your thoughts of being happy.

Explain the basic principles of what it takes to maintain a happy go lucky life for you.

'Poetic Wisdom for Life'

Encourage Yourself

The moment in time where inspirations grow, fantasies are enhanced, and truths are not deceived.

The mind travels to a surreal place in which truth isn't blind or denied— some few seconds of reality given up and extricated in Euphoria.

A place and time where opinions fall upon pure love, and pleasures doesn't succumb to the bad moments which one has created with negativity.

You find your space— live in your moments and be all that you can be— regardless of any situation, you be great.

You can love yourself like no one else has— and spread that love to others while the space you share may help you all to expand.

You can dwell in your happy place— live life and let people live according to their own will.

You don't have to be stuck and you're not fearful— you're fearless— you need to strap on for the ride that will take you to happiness.

You can find your space and let your light shine— as you have these words within you— use it every day as you rise, shine, and stimulate your mind.

Be lifted in euphoria and dwell in your positive space.

Extricate – Free yourself, be released from entanglements.

If you're ever intertwined with thoughts of what to do next.

Where to go? Who to talk to? Who to trust? While also wondering why you're so confused? Just stop and find your space, and do what you must do to succeed.

Encourage yourself by writing a poem about yourself, or write a paragraph about your future goals, your family life, your past, or however you feel.

Simply write some encouraging words about yourself on the next page.

'Poetic Wisdom for Life'

Lover's vs Friends

What boundaries— I think to myself— there are none— we're bonded together with passion.

Like sweet water from a far-away place of freshness that's not offered to just anyone— our aftertaste is pleasant, not bitter— it's pleasing to our souls.

But am I single— married— or just a great comfort zone— containing so much love but is it real love— or just delightful thoughts of what could've been us.

Who are we— show me— let's be who we need to be— on a scale of one to ten— I know that I'll be at the top of your list— I'll rank high because we're best friends.

However again— are we lovers and friends, or are we best friends only— no crossing the lines of taking things further— let's identify us and make a mend.

No more infatuations— let's make it clear— no secrets or concealed behaviors— just honesty and clear views of how we appear.

Let's live— laugh— and love as we progress— but first we must correct the defects of what's happened to modify our existence.

Have you ever crossed the lines of a platonic friendship that somehow continued to thrive even after unexpected intimacy issues? Even if you haven't, some friendships can last even through the toughest times, because genuine love and respect over rules everything.

Do you have a best friend? If so, who? And how and why are you best friends?

Some may say. "Well, I don't have a 'best friend', I barely have any people at all that I like to communicate with regularly." Use the space on the next page to describe the company that you keep, or don't keep.

Even if you feel like you don't have any friends at all, use the space to explain your thoughts about that. And if you usually assemble with a lot of friends that you trust, jot down what makes them all who they are to you.

'Poetic Wisdom for Life'

Blessings and More

Everyone faces challenges— it's common— it's a part of life that we must endure.

It's no one's desire to fail— but if you do— pull from your mental ability to understand that failing is sometimes required to help get you to more.

But rather than be scorned and allow setbacks to corrupt your soul.

Evolve and let your blessing's come gradually, as you accomplish your goals— and keep releasing good energy to others, because it helps to cleanse your soul.

Troubles don't last always, so look up— hold your head up and take heed that your attempts to succeed will indeed be another blessing received.

Standup and go for what you want— encourage yourself every step of the way.

Be ordained with good fate— while being anointed and establishing a plan— you're designed for a purpose, so just keep growing.

Invest in your own commands— with limited restrictions or doubts from your past— count your blessings and be grateful— while being alive is your blessing number one.

When a person says to count your blessings, they aren't necessarily saying that you should literally sit down and begin at number one and try to count your blessings because that's impossible.

But when you look over your life, you'll see that troubles don't last always. So this poem was inspired by thoughts of being grateful for who we are, and for what we already have as we work to earn more.

How often do you give thanks for what you already have? And what does that look like? Do you kneel and pray to God? Do you help the homeless? Do you volunteer at nursing homes, pay tithes, or etc.?

Everyone has their own ways of giving back, so use the space on the next page to explain how you count your blessings and more.

'Poetic Wisdom for Life'

Satellite Vision

Staring upon the sky as it beholds the power that revolves around the planet— the sun, the moon, the stars— read all about it, astronomy is important.

Things launched into orbit is interesting— top secret— private— only a few knows the truth about the developments of certain things.

How does it work— where do we all stand— figuring out how to pay our bills— that's our distraction, that's our attention span.

Only the universe knows the formation of its own plans— scientist work to figure things out, while we use natural products— and should eat only what we can grow.

Nothing processed— generic— because there's so much to watch out for.

Governmental facilities watching over us as we produce more— we see things in plain sight— no satellites needed, because they don't really hide— they just set rules and we follow their guidelines.

Inferior but worthy— so many of us don't know our worth, so we duck and hide, we turn away and pretend to be blind. Subordinate ourselves, and become mediocre and stuck in a commonplace.

Let's rise up and become determined— represent and take control of our space.

Like an asteroid coming in strong— be superior and dominate.
Let's use our powers and good vision to help each other out, because together no one can stop us or mess with our strong faith beyond satellites.

How do you feel about satellite vision?
In your mind, how does it all work? Who's really calling the shots in your world? Who's really making good vision decisions?

We leave the astronomy of it all to the scientists that deals with the material universe beyond the earth's atmosphere. But in your opinion, concerning our everyday life on this planet. Use the space on the next page to describe your vision.

'Poetic Wisdom for Life'

Your Will Be Done

I search for wisdom— they say it is in the quality of knowledge— understanding.

I search for peace— they say it is in nature— forces at work throughout the universe— freedom is peace.

I search for happiness— they say it is within you— a state of tranquility, serenity— being delighted, pleased, fortunate and lucky is me.

I search for money— they say it is in your work ethics, your actions and your endeavors— your attempts to survive by first being smart with money.

But, too much of anything can be harmful— so spread out and be fruitful. Be kind and help people as you find what you search for.

Too much wisdom— they say it stops us from listening to good advice.

Too much peace— they say it stops us from speaking out— you're voiceless.

Too much happiness— they say it causes us to forget those who aren't as happy.

Too much money— they say it obstructs the value of why we matter.

Discover who you are and forget about what they say— your wisdom, peace, happiness, and your money will all come with experience.

Use it all wisely— as you discover who you are as your will be done.

What has been your experience in becoming who you are today? One of your toughest obstacles happened when? And how did you survive it as you live to speak about it today?

Our good and bad experiences are necessary, it's like a needed wall forming a base for construction that will dispense needed information for us to look back on. And be able to help ourselves and others in the future with our knowledge.

Through it all, what is your current will to be done?

'Poetic Wisdom for Life'

Purest Air Moments

Dwelling in a conscious mind as I lay beneath the warm bright sun, so vibrant in its colors— admiring its rays and with the wind blowing so gently upon my face.

And as I inhale the purest air—it travels down my body reviving me as I lay— my spirit is so calm and resting in a happy place.

It's the time of year where peers come out and play— we smile— we laugh— and we party. While indulging in our joys and not stressing about tomorrow.

There's always a time and a place to have fun and cheer— this is that moment— we live in paradise and imagine that we're on the road to eternal bliss.

Supreme happiness with joy and contentment— a heavenly place of no regrets.

A place of beauty during a time of delightfulness— the season is perfect— everyone loves it here.

Feeling emancipated and freed of everything while accepting irresistible splendor— this time of season is everything, so enjoy it my dear.

A gorgeous appearance with magnificent light— grandeur in its presence, I want to live more and experience more of this good seasoned summer life.

Do you have a favorite time in your life? A time that stands out more than other times as you feel exalted in every way. When you feel balanced, free and pure happiness even if it's a bad weather type of day, you still feel joyful and happy.

We're all different, but these purest air moments are for everyone, moments when we take a break. A breath of fresh air type of day.

Use the space on the next page to express your fondest moments of joy such as you've read above regarding my purest air moments. We live, laugh, love, and should do it with a smile! Talk about the purest air moments that has made you joyful and happy inside!

'Poetic Wisdom for Life'

Show Me

Frolicking around as laughter penetrates our space— hello beautiful— your body language says while gaining attention and being more present in my face.

Wanting to kiss my cheek— you seek to try me— but you're still too afraid to reveal yourself, you must come out and stop hiding.

Now or later— if you want it then show it. Communicate your thoughts— show up and talk about it.

No more seclusion or solitude— stop your ways of being isolated— don't be stuck. Let people know what you want.

Be direct upfront and honest— but don't force it— strongly show your love, pay attention but don't overdo it.

There's no connection in silence— or at least not right now— so be forthcoming with your feelings, and let go of that blockage that you may be feeling.

Having feelings of wanting to connect with someone that you're fond of, but you're too shy, or you're too afraid to let them know. That may cause you to miss out on some great opportunities if you don't speak up.

Whether you're single or married, rich or poor, confused or clear about what you want, you must speak up.
Communicate and show people how you feel, talk as well as show up, because your actions should speak just as loud as your words.

Use the space on the next page to talk about your experiences in wanting to speak up, but you were too shy or too afraid to speak up.

Do you feel like you may have missed out on a great opportunity by being this way? If so, what would you have done differently?

But if you've always spoken up, and you're never shy or afraid to say or show how you feel. How did you develop this way of being?
Do you feel like you were just naturally born that way?

'Poetic Wisdom for Life'

Addiction Free

Ravished with fuel I now detox my body— to burn out this flame— I thought I would go deeper, ruined, and end up even less embodied.

Only to discover that detoxification was always near, to settle for less is now what I fear.

Having that thriving sickness that only poison can soothe— but with time the intoxication consumed will all be gone away— yes away as I make my way to better days.

Blooming into a beautiful flower is what I look forward to— no more controlling me with toxic waste— horror— and gloom.

Delivered from poison— alert— and candid in presenting my freedom.

I'm straightforward and outspoken about my detoxification— sincere and informative— that's my goal, that's my addiction free will.

Reserved for more— I no longer declare war against my body— because I love myself, and I'm worth more than that addiction pain and sorrow.

I'm now elevated and not intoxicated— the power is always within me— although I'm not perfect. So even when I mess up, the goal is to keep moving forward.

Never beat myself up— because that's going backwards, and that's where I don't want to be. I'll choose to keep working hard, and loving my freedom.

Have you ever had to deal with an addiction? Drugs, food, sex, money, etc.

Maybe a family member or friend has affected you with their addiction. Use the space on the next page to write about your experiences with addictions, and even detoxification.

Some people will admit that they struggle every day with addictions, while others have addictions that they aren't aware of because they don't realize that they're actually addicted to certain things.
Do you know of anyone who is unaware, or is just in denial about their addiction(s)?

'Poetic Wisdom for Life'

Narcissistic Personality

I waited under the stars— stared into the sea— I marveled in darkness— I waited for you to change, but during the process I lost me.

Endless tears spilled— how did I get here— I let your narcissism and your selfishness rule me.

If I loved myself as much as you love your self-centeredness— I wouldn't feel like a useless rock— a large mass of hardness deprived of my own thoughts.

In a relationship filled with fear— too afraid to disconnect because I'm scared to be by myself.

But being under your spell is no longer my thing— I choose me— my mental, physical, emotional, and financial responsibilities all belong to me.

Mental steadiness from now on is how I will be— you no longer scare me.

I pray— gain strength— and now I look forward to the way I adore me. Surprised by my strength and my confidence— I feel blessed.

I can't believe I let your authority become a force over me— but it's okay now. Because I have the power— I control me.

Getting out of an abusive relationship of any kind can be a struggle, so much so that there are many people who know that they are in a bad situation, but they remain due to several different reasons.

Have you, or do you know anyone who is or have been in an abusive relationship? If so, how did you or they survive it?

And as far as you know, what is the best advice that you can give to a person who is in an abusive relationship? Even if they have 'good reasons' for staying such as financial support, or they stay strictly because of their children. Whom they may be hurting even more because children can see and feel the misery even when adults pretend that they can't. And some people stay in relationships although they're being abused, but they're not getting physically abused so they excuse bad behaviors.
What are your thoughts?

'Poetic Wisdom for Life'

Break the Chains

Embodied but destitute— their diminished skeletal walks in chains. Everyone is certain of their character, but being inhibited seems to be a comfortable base.

Gleaming with soft skin— its camouflaged— reduced and restricted from the outside, and even more locked within.

No self-control— no leader— just followers— spending money and time and still not respected or believed to be worth anything.

It's time to break the chains— release the grips of reduction— you're smarter and worth more than that.

Treat yourself to a power session— it's no illusion— your light bulb has come on.

Lift your presence and do what's right— elevate and be more present now.

And even more than that— show yourself that your time is important— all you must do is honor you, and don't take no for an answer.

Respect yourself and others will respect you too— and who knows, they may even begin to follow your lead and change themselves, too.

You can break the chains and release all burdens— and gain confidence while you rise and shine above any confinement.

Are you, or do you know someone who is bound and chained?
Mentally, physically, emotionally, financially, etc.

How can someone really break the chains of a systematic thought process?

It can be difficult for people to break the chains of whatever's holding them down due to apprehension, or simply just honestly not knowing how to break the chains.
And since it's not always easy to just break the chains and be free from certain people or things, use the space on the next page to share your thoughts of what steps to take to become unchained to someone or something that a person doesn't want to be chained to.

'Poetic Wisdom for Life'

Power Through

Never underestimate even the smallest human— for even they can destroy a giant with the proper knowledge.

Expand— gain— and even train yourself with the understanding of how to use your intellect to attain, as well as maintain balance that won't constrain you into being stretched and utmost contained by stress.

Understand that to win a battle is not always measured by your appearance.

Your brain is your weapon— use it to prove strength to yourself and to others who may need to see your power.

Don't be deceived— believe that you are one of God's children.

No hesitations moving forward— the smog is gone— seeing through deception is just another milestone.

Renewed and refreshed— you should feel blessed— because loving yourself is one of the strengths to controlling your power through moments.

Life doesn't get better, you get better, so continue to gather your strength.

What do you love? What makes you happy? How do you maintain peace?

Powering through heavy times and never settling for anyone who doesn't help your growth is a great thing, because your strength will grow in the moments when you think that you can't go on. But you keep going anyway. Especially when you have strong and positive people around you, but you must power through even if you don't have people supporting you.

It's never too late to pray as you live the life that you're proud of, and if you find that you're not proud of your life.
You can reset yourself while you pray and be more active in gaining the strength that you need every day.
Five years from now, you want to be able to look at your life and say that you chose your life, you didn't just settle for whatever was the easiest ways.

How did you manage to keep control over your life this far? And how will you continue to succeed?

'Poetic Wisdom for Life'

Wake Up and Be Great

Early in the morning what's the first thing you do— your mind is free— no clutter with yesterday's opportunities.

It's a new day, a day of new beginnings— how does it start— how do you plan it?

The sun is free— shining bright and bringing light to everyone it meets— illuminating the sky with its illustrious being.

Wake up and go outside— let the wind beat against your skin— open-up and be enlightened— let your achievements sink in.

Soar like the birds and realize what life's all about— recognize your worth— you're smart, attentive, and especially aware of your importance.

Growth, celebration, and survival— being here is a revival— a restoration of life, strength, and more days to provide a healthy lifestyle.

Established and knowing what matters— don't stay sleep— wake up and be conscious— be productive and great.

This is the only way to be— woke— alive— as you're awakening is free. You're present and magnificent, you deserve to be all that you can be.

Praying is my first action every morning when I open my eyes, it's a habit, and I enjoy it because it helps me to be all that I can be.

What empowers you? When you wake up every day, what's the first thing that you do?

We all have different ways of waking up to be great. Use the space below and on the next page to write about how you rise and shine.

Oftentimes, our first actions in the morning sets the tone for the entire day. Even the foods we eat can sometimes determine if we're going to have a good or a bad day. What are your thoughts?

_____
_____
_____

'Poetic Wisdom for Life'

Love Flow

Days apart, yet I cannot forget your lips— your eyes of romance— the silhouette of your body underneath the moonlight.

I love your eyes when they flirt with mine— just as I love your arms as they're my safe-haven— big and strong.

I want to know you beyond your being— your only lover— and that goes without saying, I want soul ties, not just to be your lover and your friend.

We can conquer it all with our sweet sensations— our souls are already connected— touching each other physically is great. But lately our mental space feels perfect.

Nothing bad can stand a chance with us— because our strong flow of love over rules obstacles.

When it comes to your warm sensual seduction and great taste— nothing is more direct— fulfilling— and as satisfying as your unconditional love for me.

Sometimes it can be difficult to describe how deep your love is for someone. This love flow written above is an example of describing a connection of being close to a special person that makes you feel good even when you're far apart.

Have you ever felt such a deep connection to a person that you felt like your souls were connected? Even if it wasn't physical, describe your feelings.

Use the space on the next page to share your happy thoughts of who that person is. Explain how they became so close to you.

Share your experiences of how your love flows and how does it originate to such a personal connection.

That warm cozy feeling is essential when we're in need of some deep love flow, because life can be hard sometimes. And giving out and receiving genuine love can definitely make those difficult times much easier to overcome.

'Poetic Wisdom for Life'

Illusion Lips

Sharp like a knife are thorns that comes from his mouth in the form of words.

He loves me— he loves me not is no longer a question or a wondrous tale— those sweet soft lips that I'd kissed and grown weak upon.

Is truly no longer a questionable fairytale, but an impression of misleading trails— feeling cursed upon your touch was never the plan.

The sweetest apple ever tasted— quickly rotten and produced deceptive juices that made me sick.

I fell into a trap, I thought, until I realized it was all a psychological war.

Your mind is unstable, and your lips are poison— lethal— and they make you very abnormal. But that is you, not me.

I live to uplift, not spread hate or to intimidate— so as I leave, I'll continue to pray.

Pray for you and for me— and for this entire world because with prayer, trust, and honesty— maybe we can succeed in our needs.

I must seek to be amongst people that can really enjoy a pleasant and happy me, no more fake happiness or being in your world of delusional crappiness.

Sometimes the closest person to you can be your main thorn, and it can be heartbreaking because your love for them is genuine.

My experience of seeing that I was in a psychological war, came about after feeling so loved, but soon realizing that it was all an illusion because that same loving person seemed to be uncomfortable with seeing a smile on my face.

Have you ever experienced being in such a difficult situation? Until something happened, and then you realized in hindsight that the person was never good for you or your well-being anyway.

Explain your thoughts and experiences on the next page.

'Poetic Wisdom for Life'

Think Tank

Apply pressure while encouraging— balancing— and making a living. Take risks while making positive decisions.

Footsteps of progression frees future barriers— you will be what you strive to be— a sequence of hard work, cared for and loved on by your peers.

With qualities of communication— let's talk more— conversations are needed— and since actions can speak louder than words, exertion is what we seek.

Keep moving and accomplishing things while you continue to reach your peak— do you and keep up, you can even write down what you need.

Don't stop until you get it— even on hard days pick up this book and take in what you need— encourage yourself by reading what you're about to write and read.

Use your message for more strength— think of how great your own advice will be, as you can use this and your own words to power up and succeed.

Narrow restrictions are no more, no more indeed— you are now and will continue to be. A strong thinking tank— filled with knowledge and positive energy.

How often do you ease your brain throughout the day? Meaning, to sit quietly with little to no noise around you. No phone, television, radio, etc.

Sometimes we get stressed because our brains are constantly taking in so much as we move throughout the day.

Do you ever take at least five minutes out of your day to just rest your brain as it leads you through life? If so, explain on the next page why you take five minutes to regroup, or do you take more or less than five minutes doing this?

Maybe you feel like you don't even have five minutes to give from your day to spend time by yourself quietly. If so, do you want to change that?

Think of yourself as a think tank. How do you keep it going?

'Poetic Wisdom for Life'

Spiritual Connection

Feeling myself being spiritually connected to you— your grace falls upon me like shooting stars— I feel blessed as my feet are becoming stabilized.

I know I'm in love and it's all because of you— the security that I see in your power runs through me.

All signs lead to forever, as I freely give myself to you and you've protected me.

Only you know my destiny— because you're the one who tests me thoroughly, you're the Lord almighty.

My divine inspiration— a supreme being— surpassing excellence, you are everything.

I love you and I hope that this will always be an appropriate praise— because I appreciate the unconditional love that you have for me every day.

There will be no end to this heavenly blend— for you are with me— and your words will endure forever within me.

Your pursuit was bigger than my resistance— so I thank you for carrying me— your love saved my life and my family.

I was blind but now I can see— and there's nothing that can end our destiny. I'm a part of you and you're a part of me.

During hard times, I remember in the bible where it says. "Do not fear, for I am with you; do not be dismayed, for I am your God. I will strengthen you and help you; I will uphold you with my righteous right hand."

Do you have a spiritual connection to anyone or anything? We're all entitled to feel however we want to feel, and I feel that my faithful relationship with the Lord is my best spiritual connection.

What or who is your greatest spiritual connection?

_____
_____
_____

'Poetic Wisdom for Life'

Skin Color

Skin is our outer coating that keeps our beauty in-tact— but what do you see?

How much do you love your skin? How lovely are you? Is it smooth or is it rough? Is it brown, beige, or the color of the words on this page?

Whatever it may be— your beauty is within you— and it's up to you to see your great qualities manifest through every beautiful feature.

We are fabrics of love— our skin is a sheer mixture of a delicacy that is supposed to protect us.

Skin can be complicated— skin can be viewed with hate— fear— love— hope— and respect.

But skin is just the framework of what's inside of us— that's why the construction of a negative mind can measure the worth of how you see others and yourself.

Love for self isn't about our décor outside skin— let's love others like we should love ourselves. Show respect— gain it— and teach the youth how to love from the outside like we should from within.

This poem was inspired by the unique differences of our skin, as we all may have experienced that no matter what race, creed, or gender we're in. How you feel about yourself is most important, and our equality of having respect for one another is a message of growth and good fortune.

What has been your experiences of being in the skin that you're in?

Good, bad, pretty, or ugly. Use the space below and on the next page to describe your feelings of what a person's skin color means to you. Even if it means nothing more than just that, a skin color, because it truly doesn't matter what color a person is.

It's what's on the inside that matters? Or is that just smoke screen talk, because skin color does matter in this world that we live in?

'Poetic Wisdom for Life'

Evolve

Love is powerful— it can break us— split us open and remove all forms of life.

It can dry us out like decayed meat drained of its blood—discolored darkness and distorted of proper support.

The sun may never shine.

Then something happens— you can rise— evolve— as the sun shines and feeling disconnected and lost is no longer an option.

It's now patch me back together piece by piece— I still have life in me— now passionate affection is what I seek.

There's no more vulnerability.

It's now emit positive love and bringing forth greatness— no more lost love and tedious hatred.

Evolving into more is profoundly sacred— it's important that my space is shared with those who are just like me, those who want to make it.

Throughout the good and bad— it can be hard to appreciate life— especially when you're not mentally ready to evolve into being more than just being alive.

Love can send us on a roller coaster of emotions, love for a person, place, or thing.

How do you evolve when it has you in a funk? Or have you never been in a love funk?

Use the space on the next page to explain your experiences of how you've learned to evolve.

I've learned from my experiences to be patient while I gradually develop into who I want to be. Love has broken me, but it has also lifted me as high as I've ever been. Explain your experiences with the power of love while you move toward evolving into even more.

'Poetic Wisdom for Life'

My Muse

Joy devours you, greedily you engulf it and happily release it onto us voluntarily.

And without expecting compensation for your delighted source of energy— your mellifluous voice relinquish kindness anytime needed.

Your smile penetrates my heart and illuminates my soul— as I feel a spark of a thousand stars shining as one.

There's more than an afterglow— my body suddenly grows wings as I convey into the sky.

I soar like a bird because you make me feel that high— and with you as my muse I know I'll go far.

I live in peace and believe in the highness that you've stored upon me.

I just want you to know that you mean so much to me— and this poem is just a reflection of the greatness that you've already shared with me.

Do you know anyone who is filled with joy and creativity quite often?

Every time you see them they have a certain flair about them that brings out the good in you no matter what.

Are you that person? That bright ray of sunshine that makes yourself and others want to smile all the time.

Or are you the opposite, because you can barely tolerate people who are always joyous and upbeat all the time? Do they annoy you?

My muse are my feelings of inspiration towards the people whom I feel that's filled with joy, and inspires me because they are always spreading their love to me and others.

Use the space below and on the next page to write down your thoughts about such a person.

_____
_____

'Poetic Wisdom for Life'

A Mother's Love

The genius part of us that presides over our lives— our reasons to want to be all that we need to be, and all that we dream to be.

More than just a Mom, your presence is important like the sun— like our food— and even more so because I'm weak without you.

You're a power source— you are the strength that bestows confidence.

Better than a trophy you provide life— a daughter birthed from another great mother— it's amazing how you help with the circle of life.

Your gift to the world is more than we can see— a mother's love is the best feeling in the world— from birth to eternity.

See, even if you were adopted— given a different parent from God— cherish what you have because you've been provided with love.

A father's love is special— again cherish what you have— love your mother and your father, whomever is there providing you with love.

But this right here is for all the mother's— here's a S A L U T E to all Mom's here and the ones who are now in heaven. All grandmas, sisters, aunts, and daughters.

I salute a woman's love even if you aren't a mother— your love holds great weight— so just remember that we're a force when we're all together.

Write something about your mother, even if that person didn't give birth to you. Write something special about the person whom you consider provided you with such care as 'A Mother's Love'.

During the production of this book, I spoke with someone who didn't have anything good at all to say about her mom, or any other women in her family. And while keeping that in mind, if you have unpleasant feelings concerning your biological mother's love. Explain your thoughts on that issue, and how it can be fixed.
And if you don't want to fix it, why not?

_____

_____

'Poetic Wisdom for Life'

Don't Wait

We live off of circulating funds and exchanges— paper currency— coins and demand deposits, that's money.

Do they wait for it? I ask myself while I wait for it— the measurements of wealth, how important is it?

The gateway of life— or is it possible to comfortably live without money? Borrowed, loaned, and cashed out.

No land, investments, or even your own house to live in— what capital or currency will you use to help you and your family in the future?

Faith— love— and hope, will the integrity of our moral character provide us with what we need?

Only God knows our destiny— so along with our prayers how do we prepare to get what we seek?

I'll wait seems to never be the right choice for me— especially if I'm impaired and need someone else's dividends to provide for me.

Why wait is now the language I speak— get money is what I tell the communities. Because waiting for help is a choice that can keep you poor and asking others for their money— don't wait is the moral of this story.

I remember when I was told that money is the root of all evil, and understanding that concept wasn't hard. Although without money, you and your family could starve to death.

Therefore, I feel like it's the **love** *for money that can turn some people bad. Because some will steal, kill, and destroy whomever and whatever due to how much money actually does matter in this world today.*

But overall, money, power, and respect seems to be the good way of life. Especially when you throw in some moral values and positive actions that can help others to get their own money too.

What has been your experiences with money? Do you wait for it, or do you do whatever you must do within reason to get as much of it as you can get?

'Poetic Wisdom for Life'

<u>Why Wait: Funds Allowed.</u>

A demonstration of guiding principles is what's used to soothe and display gratitude for my peers when their seeds are manifesting and being a blessing.

Wise— unspent and powerful— with a substance of endless inspirations that makes the next generation get on board and celebrate how used knowledge is their way to elevation.

Not just filled with unused quotes— worthless written out. Funds allowed is supported— it gives power to those who want it.

No more questions of can I make it— now endless days of profits and traditional ways of working— no turning back now is our new direction.

To be alive and well— waiting has become nonexistent.

Why wait is the question? Don't live in a bubble filled with lonely struggles— only to be eventually popped by those who would rather see you sink and drown in relentless suffering.

Rise above the frustrations and those who want to see you without.

Live, laugh, love— but stay conscious of your money, and don't be taken over by debt and unappreciated love.

Funds allowed is now what we focus on.

No turning back now is my way to gaining more. What's yours?
Funds allowed is about getting your own, but only if you work for it.

Suffering due to consistent financial instability is a struggle that can hurt your whole family. Being unstable financially can take a hit on us mentally, but today we must work to fix any money management issues.

Express your thoughts on how to keep funds allowed as we rise above any money issues as of today. I had to discipline myself and stick to my small budget no matter how bad I wanted to fit in with others, I had to work smart with what I already had, and now I'm smarter with even more today. What do you think our main issues are in this society concerning the way that people manage money as far as you know?

'Poetic Wisdom for Life'

BRAIN FOOD

Machine Being

How much more transparent does it have to be to see that some humans are like machines— resembling human beings but does mechanical routines.

We must resist controlling traps of supplies and demands, and take a stand, while gathering our own mass production of supplies and demands.

Let's take on a firm position about everything— stand our grounds like the human beings that we're worth fighting for and we will win.

Don't be a machine— grab and hold on to life because God made us humans for a reason.

Alluding to a robot is not something that we should do— giving our all to our children, our job, family and friends. That can be good but be careful with that kind of machinery type of living.

Be kind, be polite, and let's give what we can. But let's not be a robot for people so much that we never pay attention to our own ways of needing and being a real human being.

Our veins are real— and our brains aren't made of steel.

No more tear drops or thoughts of doubt— as we're free to spit out that not so sweet taste of oppression, and really live without controlling attachments.

Overall, what do you think of what you just read?

Do you feel like some people live like robots? They have mechanical routines that stops them from producing their own supplies and making their own demands as human beings.

If you feel this way, use the space on the next page to express your opinion on how to change that.

And if you feel that it can't or won't ever be changed, why not?

Maybe you really don't know anyone who acts like a machine, or does things for everybody but themselves. — Let me be the first to tell you that it's a sad sight to see.

'Poetic Wisdom for Life'

Early Morning Pursuit

It's still dark— what happens— still dreaming— what's next— thinking about life while waking up and preparing for work when day breaks.

Maybe you have no job, no work, no play— a trapped mind, body, and soul— but day light awakens and brings light unto what can be a prosperous day.

Get up, clean up, and be who you are— the world is huge— it can still be yours.

Reach out and grab it— it's not easy, but you can behold it.

What happens next is totally up to you not to ignore it— it's time to get up and really get what's yours.

Oftentimes, it's said that the early bird gets the worm.

What is your perspective on that statement? Do you feel like getting up early to go after what you want is best? Or does it not matter because working smart not hard is the best way, even if you prefer late mornings?

A lot of people whom I spoke to about the process of what happens when they wake up every morning; they said that their bodies are just used to getting up early, so they really don't need an alarm clock anymore. Even on some weekends when they can sleep in, their bodies won't allow it, so they consider themselves to be early birds.

Are you an early bird?

Write down your morning routine if you have one, and if you don't have a routine that's okay. But why not?

Share your thoughts of what a person who's looking to have a prosperous day should do if they're struggling with what to do first.

What does waking up and getting started look like through your prosperous eyes?

_____
_____

'Poetic Wisdom for Life'

Amplify Me

Exhausted with clamorous thinking— emotional abuse is highly addicting— perhaps like drugs with excessive feelings. You weren't good for me.

Illustrating a shortage of intelligence— what's your cerebral approach to problems? Perhaps to magnify your abnormal principals and increase your state of being.

Good thing I've intensified my current ways of life by listening to myself— yeah the voice inside of me that told me to get up— move my feet and be amplified today.

No more false hopes or abusing my feelings— more like a better sense of being, heightened by important features, better known as my own importance.

Help make me better, don't tear me down— although it doesn't matter now, because I have someone who respects me like I respect me now.

And we never try to tear each other down.

We're increasing our strides as we're characterized by how we abide— marked and distinguished by our attributes of wanting more love.

Together we are great sources producing amplified strength, kindness, and even more love.

Specified in how we carry ourselves— our presence is evidence— proof that anything can happen, all it takes is a little finesse.

But when there's no compliance— no indications of a better notion— remember sometimes you must let people go, because warning does come before destruction.

Have you ever been in a situation where you knew that you had to release yourself from it, because it was filled with false hopes and no intentions of amplifying you or anyone else?
Use the space on the next page to also describe your experience(s) with being genuinely amplified by something or someone. What was that experience like, and are you still connected as of today?

'Poetic Wisdom for Life'

Loneliness

I feel like I live through a peep hole— am I secluded— remote from places of average human habitation.

Am I lonesome, deserted, isolated— far apart is not the life that I anticipated.

Space is needed— no questions asked— but to live null and void, and with no companionship is such a drag.

I don't need anyone is just a friendlessness brag— sometimes all it takes is a hug and a kiss to have a change of mind.

To release that aloneness, you must experience company— and it doesn't matter how many, just get around some company.

Get around two or three— but there's no rule that says a specific amount is needed.

But if you're happy to be alone— then you're great to be however you want.

Because sometimes just because you're alone, that doesn't always mean that you're lonely.

Do you ever feel lonely? Even when there are people around you, do you still feel like you are all by yourself?

If not, great, use the space on the next page to explain how you never feel alone. And why.

But if you have ever experienced feeling secluded, isolated from everyone for whatever reasons. How did you get through those moments?

Do you feel like it's OK to be alone sometimes, or do you feel like it's boring and very uncomfortable being alone?

Some people feel like it's scary to be alone, and they would do anything to assure that they're always around someone.

Are you that person? Or do you know of anyone experiencing the fear of being alone?

'Poetic Wisdom for Life'

You, Me, Us, We

Not a fictionalized hero— a real hero who gives life— we're healers with powers to restore life.

A guiding light, forever shining bright.

Not a God, but a blessing from God— you are— I am— us— we are all blessed.

Even when we're miles apart— we can rise above any darkness and push forward.

Some of us are disobedient— but we're human, we continue to work on ourselves and hope for the best outcome.

Mistakes are inevitable— you, me, us, we. All make mistakes, but learning from them is what we should seek.

However, as we proceed, our actions are important to show how much we care about the progress of our planted seeds.

We learn from the best— our ancestors were great— but would they be happy or disappointed with the directions that we've taken?

Provided with knowledge, let's use it wisely, after all— a lot of kids are watching.

What exactly are we showing them?

You, Me, Us, We was written with thoughts of how we should stick together because we can all be heroes in our own ways.

A blessing from God is who we all are, so use the space on the next page to write about how great we are when we stick together.

Also, what are we showing our youth? Are we currently sticking together as far as your opinion on life lived in your community as you know it?

Should we follow in the footsteps of our ancestors?
Do you think that our ancestors would be proud of us right now?

'Poetic Wisdom for Life'

Love Reruns

Our love symbols tattooed on my back— you were right there when the artist did that.

Now we're lost and there's no turning back— once upon a time not even anger could keep us apart.

Perhaps if you hadn't ruined it— there would still be life in what made us spark.

But like the veil that covered my face— I only saw the glares of what I thought was a perfect gift from God.

Blinded by love but now I see— so now what to do with these vivid memories— these visions of you and me that I still see.

Will you return to me is what's being asked of me— no is the answer, because accepting more disasters in my life is just no longer a part of me.

Have you ever forgiven someone so many times that your relationship was like waiting on reruns? A family member, spouse, friend, etc.

I wrote about having a relationship that seemed perfect, but was blinded by love. And when the vision became clear, there was no going back for more.

Therefore, forgiving someone is okay, but if they continue to do things that continuously have them apologizing. — At what point is their behavior no longer just their behavior? Doesn't it eventually become your behavior for continuing to accept it?

Use the space on the next page to explain your experience(s).

Sometimes people do things to show us who they really are, but when our love is blind, but strong. Some of us tend to ignore the red flags and just hope for a change, but the change never comes as we continue to make excuses and forgive bad behaviors.
Have you ever been 'blinded' by love?

What advice would you give a person who is always dealing with difficult love reruns?

'Poetic Wisdom for Life'

Love Connection

Share your love potion— attached feelings of passionate affection— profoundly tender— touched and open.

Endearment and personification is in our nature— bearing deep feelings for a parent, child, friend, or even a stranger.

Strong predilection of one another— love thy neighbor— greet them when you see them— you can even hug them.

Love can be like a drug— a habit-forming structure filled with pleasure— yet poisonous and ready for destruction.

But it can also be blessed with imbued attachment— love can be enduring— bold and capable of turning wrongs into right directions.

Breathe it— embrace it— touch it— and accept love.

And as you receive it— give it back to people just as you would love it in return.

How often do you tell your loved ones that you love them?
With so much hate in this world, it's advised that we express our feelings of love as much as we can while we can.

But even if we don't tell our family members, friends, neighbors, etc., that we love them as often as every day.
In your opinion, do you feel like your loved ones should already know how you feel by your actions, without you having to constantly say it all the time?

Being in love with love feels good, but if you're not careful it can hurt you. What advice would you give a person that is so attached to their connection that they'll accept anything to get any kind of affection?

Above, I wrote about how love can hurt you, it can be like a bad drug and destroy you. But it can also help you and lift you up, resurrect you while turning wrongs into rights.

Explain your experiences with the ups and downs of your love connections.

'Poetic Wisdom for Life'

Think It, Feel It, Believe It

I think, I feel, and I believe. What do they all have in common? Instinct.

Thoughts from the mind— feelings from the body— and belief through faith.

Think logically is what I try to do every day— sometimes it works, and sometimes it doesn't.

There's no particular order of how things should go when we're thinking, feeling, and believing in ourselves and in others.

Think positive— act sovereign and feel good inside— enjoy your life, cry tears of joy and be happy to be alive.

Order your steps in the direction of growth— believe and accept your assertions of faith— trust— and hope.

Gracefully do whatever it takes as you make healthy decisions while thinking, feeling, believing, and praying.

You are the future, and it can turn out to be however you want it to be.

Have you ever thought about doing something so much that you could feel the effects from it before it even happened?

An example of that would be like me thinking about Brain Food so much that I could feel each word before it was even printed. Because I believe in my growth and in the growth of others so much that this book has now manifested into what I thought, felt, and believed it would be before it even happened.

Use the space below and on the next page to write about your thoughts, feelings, and beliefs in how your future will be.

Can you feel the effects of it before it even happens?

As you practically plan what you want while being open and staying attentive and working smart. Explain your thoughts about your future.

'Poetic Wisdom for Life'

You and I Together

Let's elevate— rise to a higher power— a positive position promoting and placing ourselves in a present state of peace, patience, love, and hope.

Together we're strong and divided things are wrong— unresolvable— desolate and far from intelligent.

Weak versus Strong.

Let's be confident and put positivity to work— show up in our actions and keep fixing our families, communities, and more.

Let's express our thoughts whether good or bad— nothing is ever perfect— but if we start now that'll put us farther ahead.

Empathizing and compromising— that's what's important— resolving conflicts and helping each other settle our emotions.

Mutual agreeance is what it takes— no matter your race, creed, or gender— love is love— we're all the same.

Some people say that no matter how much we try and stick together, some people are going to refuse to love.
Some will even boldly speak bad things and proudly show their hatred.

Have you ever had to be around someone who hates others because of their race, creed, or gender? If so, what was that experience like? How did it make you feel? Or did you not feel anything at all?

In your opinion, explain how you and I together can make this nation so much better? And how should we handle people who refuse to be positive and helpful with promoting peace, patience, love, and hope?

It's been said that our teachings begin at home, but when there is no one really at home to learn from. Some children end up on the negative side of life due to not being taught how to properly handle their issues.

You and I together is about connecting to make this world an even better place. How do you feel about our progress as of today concerning our general direction of growth as a nation?

'Poetic Wisdom for Life'

<u>Now I See</u>

You set your eyes on me— but I've never met you— you set up an approach, introduced yourself and finally got me.

You were everything in my fantasy, but nothing in reality— a pretend life form, corrupt, void— an empty human scorned.

An image of sexiness with a bleak future— I tried to encourage you— invigorate our status and support every avenue.

No pressure, but I need stimulation too— don't lower my spirit— exalt me like I exalt you.

Stimulate my mind— or simply get away from me— I find myself having more dignity without you, I can love on me as well as those around me.

No more negativity.

I feel blessed and want the world to see— just how great life can be— when you're vigorous and opened to bigger and better things.

Because now I see that I found love in a relationship filled with hope— but I quickly found out that the invigorations was false love— but it's OK because I'm wiser now.

No more false hopes. I'm now using my experience to let you know that regardless of what you're going through— stay steady. Move forward and don't let their deceptions ruin you.

Have you ever experienced having to dismiss someone after they've mislead you or tried to lower your value?

How do you handle those situations?

And have you ever experienced having an ah ha moment because something in your brain made you suddenly see something unsettling in your sight that's been there for a while, but you were naïve, or you just simply didn't see it previously for whatever reasons? If so, how stimulating was it for you to experience the relief of knowing better and doing better? Express your thoughts on the next page.

'Poetic Wisdom for Life'

Royal Reigns

Her eyes are like magic— like glistening beams of fire— and her tears are like a thousand silhouettes of raindrops that fall beneath her eyes.

And with her watery feelings of dismay— her soaking wet shadows of fear is released through the smoke of her flaming hot eyes that allows her to be free from getting burned.

She has control— she rules her own mind, body, and soul— she's no longer stifled. She's now free to grow.

His eyes are filled with tears, but he's stuck— afraid to cry— he can't release his feelings because he's a man, and a man isn't supposed to cry.

Maybe that's a lie— he figures it out and suddenly he's revived.

Feeling free to cry and release his pain— because the truth is, at some point everyone cries when they're hurting, that doesn't make you less of a man.

And as he release his emotions— he becomes proud of himself and his big tears of joy— oh how it's helped him to maintain his life moving forward.

No more depressing raindrops of pain— even during sad times there's a bright moment somewhere for everyone— even when it's pouring raining.

Release Your Pain To Get To Your Reign.

Express yourself by using the space below and on the next page to describe how you've prevailed through pain to get to such a sovereign you.

Some of us have had some very rainy seasons in our lives.
But as frequently as they come, they go when we acknowledge it, release it, and keep moving forward.

No more stifling and suffocating in unimportant factors, don't let anyone crush you or suppress your endeavors as you surround yourself with positivity and an uplifting atmosphere is what I tell myself.
What do you tell yourself?

_____
_____

'Poetic Wisdom for Life'

__Music Therapy__

I play suitable songs when I'm mad— I sing suitable songs when I'm happy— fitting for every occasion— there's a suitable melody for every situation.

A song appropriate to alter the moment— or maybe even just the sounds of instruments is all that's needed.

Whenever mad, sad, or happy— musical rhythms are great sounds to partake in.

Good harmony and grandeur— sounds of love— spunk— and cheer.

Even without faith during certain moments of tears— music can make us feel good inside.

It can open us up— exalt us and liberate our fears.

Melodies from heaven— or right here on earth— listening to the sounds we like can be one of the best feelings on earth.

How often do you turn to music for whatever?

As you've read, music makes me feel good inside. I feel like there's a suitable song for every moment. Whether I'm mad, sad, happy, or fearful, there's a song somewhere in the universe that matches my mood and flow.

Does music have that same effect on you?

If you can relate, use the space on the next page to talk about how listening to the sounds you like helps you.

Maybe you're not very musical at all; the melodies, tones, and the rhythms of any instruments or someone singing usually annoys you.

Write down why it annoys you, or if you know someone who doesn't like listening to music. Especially when they're mad or sad, sometimes people prefer silence over anything.

What do you prefer?

'Poetic Wisdom for Life'

No Fool's Allowed

I laughed at the clown because he acted like a fool— but the clown laughed at me because I really was a fool.

I saw it too— that's why I disconnected— upgraded my thoughts and my behavior too.

A sense of pride was gained after getting rid of evilness— I can no longer be labeled a fool, and that's by myself or by anyone else who saw it too.

The respect is here— I get it— I give it— and I have the strength that I need. I pass it along to others, and they receive whatever they're ready to receive.

Unattached and messy is something that I don't agree with— do away with being immoral— it won't do anything but destroy growth.

Happy days are ahead— unfortunately some people, places, and things will have to stay in the rear.

But there's always better ways and better days to come— so look forward to even better people, places, and things that fits you and your future now.

You're great and appreciated— loved and needed— but these are just things to think about, while you realize that you are one of the greatest.

It's great when we can overcome our own self-given drama that we've taken ourselves through. Because drama and self-disappointments can be depressing, and it can destroy a person.

But when we know better we usually tend to do better, or at least a lot of us try to do better.

Have you ever had to completely detach yourself from a person, place, or thing because you began to feel like a fool?

If not, how have you managed to be who you are and help others who may not understand how to navigate their way to a better life due to them always being attached to foolishness?

'Poetic Wisdom for Life'

Connecting with Him

When you have a child like dependence on the Lord— there's a relationship between focus and faithfulness.

A supernatural being that exist with the strength of love and so much more— although some people will pledge a flag but won't pledge the Lord.

We all have our own opinions and moral rights to do whatever we want— so I pledge allegiance to the Lord, with no restrictions, just pure love.

No judgment from me for who others love— and I expect no judgment for who I love.

Life is filled with opportunities and obstacles when connecting with love— so figure out your identity and understand your natural resources.

Understanding our roles in this world today is a connection of balance and obedience that makes us a magnet to great things.

It's not all about where we're from— it's about where we're going— so having a good spiritual connection to keep us centered is a great deal of importance.

How deep was your last connection?

Whether it was with Christ, your child, spouse, parents, a friend, etc. Use the space on the next page to express your thoughts about that connection.

As you've read, I'm speaking about my connection with Christ because it's such a great feeling for me.

But some people may feel like there are people around them all the time, but no one understands them so they don't feel a connection to anyone, or anything. So they prefer to be alone, and it's okay if a person needs to take some time for themselves to figure out what's what. But they should also understand that our lives are too big to live in total isolation.

Do you have another connection other than yourself to genuinely reach out to when you need something greater than you are able to provide yourself with?

'Poetic Wisdom for Life'

Love Thoughts

Falling in love is easy— but what happens when we're fully in love— is it forever, or just a deep passing through type of lust.

Falling in love can be conceptualizing from possessions to our physicality's.

But being in love can come from a deeper feeling within— a deep connection in which a person can bring out the worst and the best in you.

Although too much love can be fatal— especially if we lose our own sense of being by loving others but resisting our own soothing love and respect for ourselves.

I love how we can be a blessing when our desires to be nurtured comes together— and the development of affection for one another attaches us to a deeper level.

That's why we should never let the anguish times from our past bring uncertainty into our future.

It can take over our brains with previous times of pain— halting our will to receive love or provide love to someone great who really wants to love us unconditionally.

Talking about love helps me because I enjoy it, it's so uplifting to think about the feelings that keeps me happy.

What has been your experiences with falling in love to actually being in love with something or someone? Was it instant, or did it take a long time before you realized that you were no longer falling, you were in love?

Sometimes love just happens. Do you believe in love at first sight? Or do you know of anyone who says that they've fallen in love at first sight, and they're still together years later?

Maybe you don't entertain any love connections at all, maybe love is just another four-letter word that has no important meaning to you.

Use the space on the next page to express your loving thoughts.

'Poetic Wisdom for Life'

I Feel It Coming

Drifting day by day and searching for inspiration to come my way— I found nothing until today.

Nature spoke and said— venture to the great outdoors and travel the less visited places.

The anticipation of life being planned out while waiting for more inspiration to come my way has me floating.

My anxiety about the future is so invigorating— because I know how I want my life to go— vitalized and full of great surprises I hope.

A twist of fate— fulfilling dreams and escaping the trickery— being captured by grace and proportioned just right will be my victory.

Extended in a magnitude of greatness— important and determined to join these views of foreseen wonders.

I feel it and see it coming— a place of satisfaction and genuine happiness.

Have you ever had a premonition, a feeling of anticipation or anxiety over your future or anything else? If so, what was your premonition and how did it all work out?

It's been said that if you expect great things then great things will happen, and if you want something then you should say it; speak it into existence. Have you ever been told that if you want something then you should claim it?

If so, did you claim it and eventually receive it?
Or has none of this ever happened to you because you've said it, claimed it, envisioned it, and almost felt it. But it still never actually happened?

Use the space below and on the next page to talk about your experiences whether good or bad.
Also, have you, or do you know anyone who loves to speak on what they want. But they don't want to work for it to actually make it happen?

'Poetic Wisdom for Life'

Don't Stop

Have you ever been tested by life? Mentally, physically, or even financially? Me too— and it seemed like I was hand-picked, and always at the wrong time— yet I still survived.

For what purpose? To have more time to live and to give and receive.

I'll never rebel and go against all that I've built— not me I tell you— I'll outsmart foolishness then turn away and dip.

Like a message in a bottle— I'm old— wise— and informative.

Have faith is what I say, because timing is everything— whatever you want, keep at it and with time you will get what you want.

Tick tock is the lullabies of the clock— the only time to stop is when we pause to enjoy bright moments with what we already got.

Time is of the essence— prepare— develop— and just get ready to pass the test of your time.

Live in your purpose because there's only one you— and your time is now.

Have you ever wanted something so bad that you went after it and nothing could stop you? But as you was determined and preparing to get what you wanted, something happened, or did multiple things happen that tried to stop you?

Did it get too overwhelming and you actually stopped?
Or has this never been your experience with stopping? If you've been tested to see how bad you really wanted something, how did you pass the test?

If you got tired of waiting and went in a different direction.
Do you now regret turning away from something that you wanted so badly?

And if you feel like you've never been the type of person to quit at anything. What does that look like?
And what advice would you give to someone who's currently thinking about giving up on something that they really want?

'Poetic Wisdom for Life'

Voting Rights

Often inconvenient— time consuming and may even seem pointless. An association of lies— some people are fed up— they say they're just over political ties.

Forget exercising our free will for a better life— our rights guaranteed by our constitution are viewed by some people as a rule of oppression in plain sight.

Is the system working for us? Are they right?

How often do you vote— is it a fair process of importance— or just unfair politics and endorsements?

Not just for a President— but for other positions seeking to be held— elected by citizens who allow them to have an important effect over our lives.

From schools, to health care, to the economy— how much do we really know— how much more should we seek?

Voting is supposed to be an important right in society— making our voices heard— registering our opinions on how things should be done.

Today you have a choice— some say choose the lesser of the two evils— while others think they're choosing a smart leader.

Either way, no matter who runs for office. Ultimately, is it really our choice? Should we vote? Does our voices really matter?

How do you feel about voting?
Better yet, how do you feel about politics in general?
In your opinion, does your voice really matter?

Some people only vote during the Presidential elections, and when bad city officials make horrible decisions, those same people who didn't vote become upset.
They speak about being angry over how some school districts are not good, they speak angrily about the Sherriff's, Prosecutors, Judges, and more.

But how do you feel about our voting process, and the citizens who do or don't vote?

'Poetic Wisdom for Life'

Drunken End

How to escape from it— bottle after bottle— it hurts— but the addiction is too strong, it's a painful liquid to let go of.

In a room waiting for despair to be in the air— a loss of self while the brain is impaired.

Liquid intoxication— it shames and it scares— it turns lives around, more so upside down.

Inevitable moments of unnecessary pain— caused by poisonous acts of overpowering sins.

Exhilaration of the mind and emotions can send us into a binge— excessive consumption of alcoholic indulgence.

High-proof water— married to fire— born into a thirst of warm rituals to herald the souls of mortals everywhere.

Fierce spirits distilled and removed from life— condensed and reduced to nothing is how it all ends.

I won't let it take me away— as I slowly let go of the pain— the thirst is no more— because the embracing of a sober reality has now taken over.

Have you ever experienced having too many alcoholic beverages? If so, how often and why? What really makes you partake in it?

Or maybe you've only had one drink and you've never drank alcohol again.

Use the space on the next page to explain your thoughts on how this firewater has effected your life.

And if it hasn't been a factor at all, explain why and how you've been able to live alcohol free. Especially the positive aspects of being who you are without it.

'Poetic Wisdom for Life'

Good Deeds

I saw a man in need so I helped him— I extended my hand as a good deed.

To my findings his thank you did not suffice— I wasn't pleased and wanted a bigger thank you for my good deeds.

Where did my good intentions lie— because it wasn't in the good graces of doing something right?

What was I expecting for my help— where was the love— because it wasn't real support if given with a fraudulent heart.

To my realization I've learned that helping is stemmed from the heart— love is free and should be given unconditionally— no faking needed.

A good gesture and feelings of appreciation is great— but after giving then looking for a return, you may end up disappointed.

Educe your love— release it without expectations of a return— thrive and be strong, because helping is a blessing born from love.

You'll get what you put out— just be patient— do good deeds and have faith in knowing that you are doing the right things.

Have you ever helped someone and looked for a return on what you've done?

I speak about having a realization of how much helping is stemmed from love, and how we shouldn't expect favors for helping and loving others.

Do you believe that if you genuinely spread nothing but love, then you'll get it back in return? And if your answer is no, and you feel that you won't always get it back in return no matter how much love you give. How do you handle situations like that where your love has been unappreciated, or not accepted in a way that you thought it should be accepted?

Use the space below and on the next page to write down a few of your most recent good deeds that you've done for someone!

'Poetic Wisdom for Life'

Physical You

I smile at how you seduce me— even your smell has a way of showing up boldly and filling the room with greatness.

The occurrences of your touch ignites the flame that burns for you— I'm intensely ready for your love to come into my life even more.

Engulfed with lust— and I like how we treat it— our physical urges are brought upon us by our hugs and simple kisses.

No sex is the ultimate question— should we wait until we're married?

There's already a physical connection— because even when I hold your hand— it's like our souls are as one every time we touch each other.

Our physical feelings are one thing— but you truly love my body, my mind, and my heart the same. And that's what's important to me.

Your love decorates me with honors of structural style— you are my symbol of love— your eyes are concealed with trust, and I really feel secure.

This attraction is good for us— mentally and physically— especially with the respect that we both share when deciding to be sexually active.

Being attracted, then closely connected to someone mentally, physically, emotionally, and even financially can change a person's life forever. Especially if it's a real love connection and the feelings are mutual.

But have you, or do you know of anyone who has been very attracted to someone, but you or they chose to wait to have sex in the relationship? If so, how was that? If not, how deep was your overall connection?

Even if it wasn't just the physical connection that got you. Have you ever been caught up in such a way as I've described above?

In a way that keeps a smile on your face and wanting to experience more. What has ultimately been your favorite attraction of mental or physical love?

'Poetic Wisdom for Life'

Mental Responsibilities

Some of the roughest people can possess hidden qualities that are blessings overshadowed by mental health issues.

With a soft or rough outside appearance— what's on the inside can be a mystery— mentally stressed or diagnosed, talk to people before you judge.

Daily living is sometimes good and sometimes bad— but having mental issues can be harder if you're always gloomy and sad.

Common ways of distress are responsibilities that we can help— provide yourself with an outlet to go to when you're feeling stressed.

The question is, are we taking care of each other when there's a cry for help— or are we too busy— maybe taking care of ourselves is already hard enough.

Some people are grand on the inside— sometimes hyper like a child— honest human beings that can also become manic, or even depressed and shut down.

With natural sweetness, or with medicated help— do whatever you need to do to keep yourself right.

Your mental responsibility is yours to keep straight—believe you can do that.

Loaded with trails of support is the goals for mental health— let's hold on tight with tough love and strength— but also with tenderness.

Have you had, or do you know anyone with mental health issues?

If so, what are the issues and how do you or they deal with it?

Some people have mental issues and don't deal with their issues for several different reasons. Some may be in denial about having issues, and some may recognize their issues, but believe that they can handle things on their own without any help.

Use the space on the next page to express your thoughts regarding your mental health responsibilities.

'Poetic Wisdom for Life'

BRAIN FOOD

<u>Dream Catcher</u>

When goals are set and determination sets in— catching your dreams are inevitable; even when it seems that your dreams are too much and too far.

You're covered with natural instincts to be whatever you want to be— be honored as you achieve your goals and rise to get even more.

With meaningful outlets like prayer— meditation— and so much more.

Why be attached and hang on to people and things that aren't good for your soul?

Be authentic and take your own road— it may not be easy— but choosing your own authenticity is the best way to go.

Rise-up— you can reach the top as you use your brain to help yourself and others to reach their dream catching goals.

Your plans are in motion— seek help and stay around positivity— as you encourage yourself every step of the way.

Achieve your success naturally without jealousy greed or hatred— measure your intentions as you stretch your ambitions and succeed.

Terminate and completely let go of anything that's preventing your dreams. While you remember that self-discipline is difficult, but it's very important to have it while you attempt to catch your dreams.

Sometimes people set ridiculous goals for themselves to reach without first using their common sense to see if it's an attainable goal to strive for.

And although I feel that no goal or dream is too big, because if you want something bad enough, and you work hard enough to get it.
Then who's to say that you won't get what you worked for.
I say, live your life and go for whatever you want because only you can stop your dreams and goals.

Use the space provided to talk about your dreams and how it's been since living it.
Or talk about how you hope to one day turn your dreams into a reality.

'Poetic Wisdom for Life'

Prosperity

Don't forget from where it stems. — Why do you want what you want? — How will you get it?

Feel free to repeat it— say it over again— take it in and keep it— it's your good fortune to get and to dwell in it.

Doing whatever you want is always within your reach— while you breathe and be provided with another day to be prosperous and happy.

Seek to live within your means— your light will shine and you'll get everything you need— no one but you can stop your prosperity.

The light within you is always on— time is merely a small distance away— because you're as far as you can visualize you are today.

Be alive and not weighed down— nor half dead and with no soul found.

Happy times are here because this is your fate— and being loyal to your supporters as well as yourself will lead you into even better days.

Take time to live, feel, give, and adopt more— you are a blessing and so is your wisdom.

The time has arrived— time to flourish— time to take advantage of who you really are— it's time to show them.

Do work and get your general and financial respect— while following your instincts and thanking God first.

I speak a lot about positivity and being all that you can be, but I understand that sometimes it can get hard when you're trying to stay positive. But it seems that nothing goes well no matter how positive you are.

Use the space on the next page to write down your experiences with the ups and downs of being prosperous in your life, throughout the good and the bad times.

What does success, flourishing or thriving conditions, and just good fortune and financial respect mean to you?

'Poetic Wisdom for Life'

Forgive and Makeup

I smelled a rose and thought of you— I picked it up and held it tight— wondering about us and why do we fight.

Hugs and kisses feels better— but our anger falls upon us and we argue— but that doesn't mean that our love is over.

The day pass and so does the night. How long is too long to go without speaking and holding each other tight?

Love is joyful— it makes us feel warm inside and happy— we feel cared for and it helps us to shine more.

I hate it when we fight— let's make up and forget about the past— deal with the problem like friends; let's start over and be us again.

We have more presence of love and absence of pain— as we realize that being hurt is just another part of this entire love thing.

Greater than a cold beverage on a hot beach, and when it's cold it's like a body being wrapped in thick but soft Egyptian sheets.

I want you close up— right here next to me— but all I have is a rose, a rose that smells so clean and sweet.

Return to me my love— let's apologize— let's forgive each other and makeup.

This poem was written with the emotions that can be felt after an argument. Have you ever had a misunderstanding, an argument, or even a physical fight with a loved one and your relationship never recovered from it?

If so, use the space on the next page to write about what happened, and how you were able to move on from that person and heal.

And if your relationship ultimately worked out, and you're still in love and moving along strongly. How were you able to move forward and stay connected after such an ordeal? And is there a limit on how many times a person can mess up and ask for forgiveness?

'Poetic Wisdom for Life'

When Turning a New Leaf

Feel the peace— you can even accept grief— embrace your strength and gain life more abundantly.

Turning over a new leaf requires trust— love— faith— and patience. Remember the past, but release the nastiness.

Any evil sins of pain— let it go— find life and feel peace while having no regrets of your failures from yesterday.

Praise and give thanks while looking into yourself to live greater day by day— one day at a time is a great starting place.

Be positive— stay aware and shed no more bad tears from those other days— you're awesome— believe in yourself today.

Never stray or talk negatively against yourself.

It's a new day— a blessed day to be thankful to see another day— so let's live, give, and encourage each other to be as best as we can be today.

Tomorrow is not promised— live life as if it's your last day— hug too much, kiss too much, smile too much, laugh too much, and love too much is what I suggest doing each and every day.

Have you ever had to turnover a new leaf? Meaning you had to change things about yourself or your situation and start over.

Voluntarily turning away from people, places, and things can be difficult.

But when you're ready to leave the old things behind that's not helping your growth, for some of us it's not difficult at all. Because when your eyes are truly opened, and you're fed up with going nowhere fast. It's not difficult to turn over new leaves, trees, and whatever else that's needed to get us to what we need.

Use the space below and on the next page to describe your experience(s) with 'turning over a new leaf'.

_____
_____

'Poetic Wisdom for Life'

I Am

Beautiful— spiritual— and strong. Versatile— wise— and generous.

I have the executive abilities to lead— but sometimes afraid to take chances and attain the necessary things I need.

I'm a breathing example of being practical by nature— a holy garden of forthright actions that can lead to uncertain ways of life.

Through broken chains of trust— I rise above— I've taken control and realized that my dreams are within me, only I can own it.

But to live and be independent takes courage— endurance— and faith.

Whether I change or remain the same— I am me and I love it because no one else gets to be me but me, so I adore my abilities to be all that I can be.

My experience is interesting— especially when I try something different, like going far beyond my normal range of living.

I am who I am— I live to spread my love— I want to help uplift, support, and be the best me that I can be to myself and to others.

I share me, my mind— my strength— and even my money— but there are a few restraints because I will never let anyone have massive control over me.

If you will, please take this time to think of who you are, then give yourself praise as you pat yourself on the back for who you are this far.

Appreciate you, take this time to honor yourself because sometimes it's hard to stop and see how truly great we are as we thrive amongst so many different people within this world.

Use the space below and on the next page to just love on yourself, and if you feel like you have more loving to do, because you haven't quite figured out how to truly love yourself. Explain how you will now begin your self-love journey.

_____
_____
_____

'Poetic Wisdom for Life'

BRAIN FOOD

Support System

My anchor— I can rely on you— my stability— I can count on you— my rock.

Holding tight and providing a firm security of being there— you are here— your actions speaks louder than your words.

When troubles arrive— they reshape into needed experiences as far as I'm concerned— because your support gets me through bad circumstances.

I need you— your heavy fix tells me to keep moving forward.

A vessel of hope— love— peace— and joy that keeps me going— a beautiful star shining bright and with powers that glow.

Your strength and support keep me upbeat— strong— and ready for more. I'm growing without chains as I claim more— and with your support— I don't divert.

And guess what— to anyone reading this who feels like they don't have any support— this poem is about me. I am my support.

I rely on me and others can see it too, so they help me and believe in me also.

And I return the favor and show them love and genuinely support them too— because we're all planting seeds and growing, and it feels good to watch each other grow.

Do you have a good support system around you? And are you a good support for yourself and for others too?

It's always good to help others, although it can be difficult to provide support for someone else when you don't have any support provided to you.

Use the space below and on the next page to talk about your support system, as well as how you've been of support to others. And if you feel like you don't have any assistance, what do you think should happen to get you more support?

_____

_____

'Poetic Wisdom for Life'

Addicted to Comfort

Unleash the comfort but don't lose it— release some of what you have to gain more— as you find your space for growth.

Never get too comfortable and settle for less— live life because comfort is found within us and not always through the actions of someone else.

Be surrounded by goodness— people who love you, trust you, and truly want what's best for you.

Although an uneasy life can force you to create— and bring upon changes that will have its own blessings and sometimes even its curses.

What I know is that being uncomfortable can leave you restlessly wandering— filled with apprehension— and squandering.

But you must release that fear— get uncomfortable and make a change. Because the time is now, today, your time to rise is here.

Addicted to comfort will have you stuck— feeling the same all the time and with nowhere to go— don't let your comfort zone have you feeling reluctant.

When something is making you uncomfortable, especially something or someone that you know isn't good for you anyway, but you remain due to whatever reasons.
That can be a very unhappy and painful life. But have you ever gotten uncomfortable in a situation, but you were happy about it because you knew that you were just getting prepared for something better? Or do you deal with being uncomfortable differently?

Describe your thoughts of being uncomfortable, and have you ever been addicted to comfort?

There's no real comfort in being in an unhappy situation, some people are so addicted to being comfortable in their unhappiness. That they would rather stay where they are, rather than to get uncomfortable and make a way for change.
No one wants to be uncomfortable for long, but sometimes we must get uncomfortable for us to get to a much better comfort zone.
Explain your experience(s).

'Poetic Wisdom for Life'

Parent Person

That pivotal moment when mom isn't mom— she's a woman— and dad isn't dad. He's a man.

They love, they suffer, they laugh, and they cry. They provide, they survive, they live, and they give. And like you— they are real.

To whom that doesn't know their parents— you are not alone— and to those who often see their parents, we all still share many things in common.

Not just a protector— a hero— or even an invisible villain for some— no love at all, just gave birth and took no time to really hold you in their arms.

Through it all whether they're away or present— a parent's love is real— even when they aren't presenting a good message.

Depending on their own childhood history— some may never be around— but you should keep living and being the best person you can be.

Don't repeat the cycle of sadness, by turning your own kids upside down.

Even with both parents always around loving and available— we're all human and learn daily— so just remember that a parent is still a person, regardless of what happened after birthing you.

How do you feel about your parents?

Some of us live our lives exactly like our parents, and some of us are totally opposite of our parents.
Even adopted children have been known to be just like their biological parents, even if they've never personally met them, but others who have met their biological parents can see it.
And some turn out to be exactly like their adoptive parents.

But no matter how or who you were raised by, express your thoughts on how you as a child, or even you as a parent can relate or not to your parents.

Is your life a reflection of how you were raised, or do you live a totally different life from how you were raised?

'Poetic Wisdom for Life'

Old-Fashioned

Earlier times were delightful— formerly known ways taught great posture— sit up straight— respect yourself and be proper.

Past times hold a lot of memories— some great— some of hate— and some want to erase the past completely.

Experience is magical— long standing and wise— mature in nature— old, advanced, and filled with knowledge— but it can be overlooked sometimes.

Far advanced in years— as life goes on and you do whatever you must do to maintain a good living and a happy structure too.

Outdated or brand new— either one is good to choose— because new is good, but old is too— prehistoric lessons last forever.

Pick and choose what you may need to use— but old-fashioned living is usually good.

Improve with time and live how you must— but never forget your elders— listen to them because they know more than we give them credit for.

Traditional ways may be a thing of the past— and that's okay to a certain extent— because times change and some things are better when done differently.

But show respect to your history and pass along the good stuff— let the bad be a lesson of what not to do— while blessing others with your good wisdom and examples of what they can do next to improve.

How often do you sit down and have lengthy conversations with your elders?

Old-fashioned ways and older people are attractive to me because of their actions, loyalty, and the respect for one another that I've been blessed to witness. New school ways are good and works for me also, but there's a balance that I had to put in place as I grow and attempt to show others what I've learned from my elders.
How do you balance 'old-fashioned' ways versus 'new-fashioned' ways of living?

'Poetic Wisdom for Life'

What's Your Pleasure?

It's pleasing to the soul in times of need— it soothes me with significant forms of relief.

Through elements of rhythm— melody— harmony— and color.

Magnetic sounds expressing ideas and emotions— oh how I love how it can bring us all closer.

Sounds occurring in a single line, the melody— or multiple lines, the harmony— we band together with glory.

Singing, hearing, and listening to the tones of all sorts of different voices— combining cultures, teaching, and producing great vocals.

Music is my pleasure— it vibrates my body— it makes me dance— I shake my head, arms, legs, and even my chest.

Everyone can relate— babies, toddlers, teenagers, elders, and all adults— from the womb we can hear music coming from this earth.

Expressing ourselves through instruments, hymns, and more— music is my love— my therapy— I use it as my support.

I'm pleasured with dancing and lifting myself up— through all of my relief efforts— music is my pleasure of choice.

What's your pleasure?

Use the space below and on the next page to talk about your experiences in how you get relief. Relief from work, school, or just life in general.

Being pleased with doing certain things can be a great stress relief, because you get to do something that you enjoy doing. Whether it's reading, singing, cooking, traveling, or whatever gives you gratification. Having a positive outlet to get some relief from is a great way to cut down on stress.

How are you fulfilled?

'Poetic Wisdom for Life'

Two as One

Share, they would say, two heads are better than one— be your brother's keeper and your sister's equal.

Even with no biological siblings— we're taught to mingle and to make peace— even if you're the only child you should still spread love and positivity.

But some strangers look at me and you and can't see— all of the great things that can happen with love and unity.

Still be you because guess what— that's all that you can be. Pray for them and move on, and don't let their lack of love affect your prosperity.

Two as one makes us equal— but only if the two agree.

And no matter how many of us there are— when we're positive and joined together to become a force— one makes we.

And having a two as one mentality— helps some of us to be strong and mighty.

And that's the thought process we need— let's help assist each other into being as great and as powerful as we can all be.

It's fun talking about change and growth, and how good it is to have positive people around us to help keep us positive.
Do you have anyone around you whom you've joined forces with as you've become a positive two as one?

If so, use the space to write about that person or those people, and how much their presence brings positivity and enlightenment to your life.

And if you don't have anyone in your life that you feel like you're close enough to say that you're united as equals. Why is that and what could happen for this to change if you want it to change, and if not, why don't you want it to change?

_____
_____
_____

'Poetic Wisdom for Life'

Food Bank

Everything edible shouldn't be eaten— let's nourish our bodies and provide good energy— let's sustain life and grow carefully.

Good water isn't always free— so being cautious of what we consume should be very important to our communities.

Especially while unpurified water and processed food is still on a killing spree.

What do we eat— where does it come from— who makes it— how many hands touch it before it gets to me?

Is it all about money— all the sugar— the sweetness entering many pockets— corporations soar while making big profits.

Why not grow our own food? A garden is a pleasant sight to see— eat of what we know— eat from our own trees as we work together to keep planting seeds.

Let's be strong and healthy— after all, not only food, but money can come from trees.

So just remember when you're hungry— some of those pretty appetizers aren't designed to nourish you— it really isn't all its potluck to be.

Just be careful of what goes into your mouth— it shouldn't be food of convenience— because the people who sell it would never eat what you eat.

How often do you eat processed foods?

I've heard people say that they don't live to eat, they eat to live. Meaning they only eat enough to stay nourished because they aren't really food fans. They understand its importance, but their eating habits are far different from some of us who often indulge in food cravings.

What is your relationship with food in general?

Do you have a lot of food cravings that you often partake in, or are you the type of person that carefully watches what goes into your body?

'Poetic Wisdom for Life'

Shadow

Trace my being beyond a shadow of doubt— I see a dark figure— an image cast upon the ground.

My reflected body image intercepting light— it's a shade of darkness— traced by my life.

Slightly faint— but like a shadow I'm sometimes absent of light.

But not today— today I'm bright— even my shadow looks radiant and filled with life.

Living happily ever after is the plans for my life— hello shadow, things are different now.

Luminous and concise is a great way to be— steer clear of negativity— be brief and quickly remove yourself from strife.

Be a shadow of power— shelter— a protector with a distinct image of strength and strong abilities to balance a powerful life.

Don't be a ghost pursued in your own shadows— show yourself more— live free and enjoy your life.

Fear can have a way of making us walk in the shadows of others, or as perceived in this poem, it can have us tracing a shadow of darkness until we renew ourselves.

So be radiant and show yourself. Never live in someone else's shadow when you can live free and be your own positive shadow of life.

Use the space below and on the next page to explain your thoughts on if you agree or disagree with it being okay to be in someone else's shadow for a moment, if that's what you need to get you on a path to happiness.

But at what point should you focus more on your own shadow to live your own life within your own true happiness?

_____
_____
_____

'Poetic Wisdom for Life'

Light Fear

When a closed mind is opened— turning on the lights can be a nightmare— and no sleep becomes the way to be.

Turning on the lights equals fear— it's adequate for being afraid— but the lights off means not having to deal with anything.

Please grasp your presence and come on— be clear.

Lights on or lights off— you should have no fear. Grow your trust and see what's in front of you, while flipping the switch to being fearless and awesome.

Brighten your day with a smile on your face— glow like a light and let it consume you all day.

The lights on and off scenario can be a tragic story— but only if you're lost and don't want anyone to find you.

Fearing the light or going toward it is a choice that we'll all have to make— how you feel and view your own story is totally up to you.

Be a light and shine bright in this world today— you only live once, so enjoy it. Be that bright light that you would love to see.

Do you ever experience those deep lights on and lights off moments?

I encourage grasping your presence and becoming clear in what you want if you aren't already clear of what you want and how you want it, because turning on the lights may be a bit scary for some people. But living in the dark is even scarier. So flip the switch to on and live your best life now.

How do you grasp your presence and come on?

Use the space below and on the next page to express your thoughts on fearing light. Do you fear it, or are you fearless, and more so gravitate to any forms of light?

_____
_____

'Poetic Wisdom for Life'

Be Patient Love

To whom is your love felt— closest to your heart and often your counterpart.

Instant protection because even through pain your love saves— it's preeminent and it's grand.

Think of true friendship— does it last— does it expand— think of whom you love, when you argue is it worth the pain?

Weeping may endure for a night— but if you hold on you'll see that after crying, your feelings will mend, and you'll be alright.

Be patient with love and examine change— allow yourself equanimity— you'll know where to be strain.

Love is patient and important enough to wait on it— because sometimes it takes a while, but it's worth the wait.

The highest rank is perhaps when it adores you— when it's responsible and loyal.

Accept love as it accepts you— everything else is just not as important— so don't be annoyed, irresponsible, or disloyal with love.

Remove hate and be gracious— because love looks good on you.

How patient is your love?

Do you quickly hug people and tell them how you feel? Or are you quick to dismiss? Not much into hugging and talking about your feelings?

Love feels good, but it can also be challenging.

Have you ever had to deal with any loving moments where your patience ran out? Even with the most genuine love felt, no amount of patience could save it from being destroyed.

Explain your experience(s) as it relates to your love and patience.

_____
_____

'Poetic Wisdom for Life'

Formal You Formal Me

Look at my eyes— I see your eyes— hear my voice— I hear your voice— observe me and I observe you.

We're separate but together— you guide me and I guide you— we're never misled. We're highly organized— generalized and simplified by our strides.

Conforming and adhering in great taste— having respect and being smart goes a long way.

A new tradition of standards has been set— we don't have to join hands, hug, or wear fake smiles on our faces.

We're established by a general consent of faith— we trust and show each other the same good energy, love, loyalty, grace, and respect.

A formal you formal me is formed and is favorable and safe— evil is always present— but we pray— live wise and appreciate our blessings every day.

It's up to you and me to stay positive— push through and try not to conform to any negative ways.

Play it safe as we make this world a better place— and it's OK to keep your eyes open and prepared for things to go in opposite ways.

Because having respect doesn't mean that problems won't come— so stand your ground and protect it, because there is no other way. But always remember that being formal and having standards will take us a long way.

Being formal can take us a long way as we ensure progress and respect as it relates to coming together as human beings.

How often do you observe the social behaviors of those around you?

As we all attempt to form, shape, and mold ourselves. We must discriminate against anyone who doesn't want to establish a formal and safe environment for growth.
What are your thoughts on being or not being more formal these days?

'Poetic Wisdom for Life'

BRAIN FOOD

Moving Upstream

Against the current— moving towards a higher part of life— let's adore it.

The transition can be distinguished and situated by our rowing ways of life— or latter pushed back and obsolete— don't be set aside.

Gaining something better— perhaps flowing water with no getting lost in the tide. How do we get there you ask? It's simple— no more free rides.

Perspiring with strength, love, and endurance— leave behind bad distractions during these voyage days.

With power waves proceeding the future— even only slightly opened eyes can gain more and have a broader existence.

Mystified bodies in discontented places— don't let nothing stop you— let's get more despite any high waters.

Anything holding us back from bettering ourselves is not our mission.

Be baptized in righteous acts— and emerged in goodness— like purified water flowing through us for good health, we're safe and healthy.

Often cleansing spiritually, mentally, and physically will indeed help us to stay happy and alive to live and give more abundantly.

Have you ever heard someone say that they're alive but they're not living?

If so, how did you comprehend what they were saying?
Some people wake up every day and that's it, they're alive of course, but they're not really living.

Use the space on the next page to elaborate on your thoughts about mystified bodies in discontented places.

I've used thoughts of moving upstream as a positive way to live if you ever feel like you're happy to be alive, but you're not living as best as you can. I always encourage people to push back and move upstream when they feel like they're drowning.
What do you use to keep yourself moving upstream?

'Poetic Wisdom for Life'

<u>Close Enemies</u>

They shine in lies and conceal their identities— they can be like the hot sun as it shines— but too much of them will burn you.

Unlike the sun— they don't live to give life— they more so try to deprive you of living your best life.

They take away your sweet warmth— they sour you— wickedly and morally wrong. Don't let them devour you.

Their mischievous actions causes more misfortunes— so release those devils and pay attention.

Rise above any hurdles of destruction— they are no longer barriers obstructing growth and causing disruptions.

The love for self is now present and ready— time to live and remain healthy.

Your enemies can't hold you, control you, or stop you.

The moral of the story is— keep an eye on your enemies— but don't let them stall you, or get too close and ultimately distract you.

What has been your experiences with dealing with defiant people?

How do you control your interactions?
Some people are just wolves in sheep's clothing as they pretend to like you, although truly within themselves they may be jealous or envious of you.

But there are several different reasons why some people possess false love, or secretly hate on others.

Use the space on the next page to express your thoughts on how to deal with your enemies, if you have any.
I have no problems releasing people from my life depending on how bad they are, but sometimes releasing people from our lives isn't always easy, even if they are bad.
Have you ever been close to someone who tried to stop you from being great, but it still wasn't easy cutting them off?
Or was it actually very easy for you to let them go?

'Poetic Wisdom for Life'

Reach Out

Having clean water to drink, bathe in, and cook with.
How healthy is it? How safe are we?

How quickly do we decrease without money? There's homelessness— abandonment and more. How do we really feel about people who can't afford clean water and other good resources?

Give back— if only a little— because some of us try hard, but we still can't afford to really live. So we must band together to gain and sustain more.

Trust each other— share our resources even with those whom we feel don't deserve it— be cautious when judging, because they just may be hurting.

Protect yourself and your family too— but sometimes you must look out for your fellow man if you can.

Although sometimes you can't— because they're too far gone and will try to pull you down.

To be around them is like sinking sand— so reach out once because you care— twice if you dare. But after that move on because sometimes you just can't help.

Let them dwell in their own demise because some people must reach the bottom before they will even attempt to help themselves.

How often do you do charity work?
In my past, I didn't do much charity work because I felt like I could barely help myself. I felt like I didn't have very much to give anyone, so I stayed to myself and would be there for anyone if they asked me.
But if they didn't ask, I didn't offer anything. Especially not any money, because I didn't really have it to give.
But I later experienced things that allowed me to see and feel how good it felt to help others even at my lowest times in life, I couldn't give money.
But I did reach out with a hug, and with spending time and having conversations with people who were less fortunate than I was.

Explain your own favorite reaching out moments that helped you and others too.

'Poetic Wisdom for Life'

DNA

A self-replicating material present in nearly all living organisms— the carrier of genetic information— a ladder like arrangement that can't be taken away.

But our fundamental and distinctive characteristics of being kind is a choice— some hate their brother, sister, father, and even their mother for reasons of all sorts.

Unchangeable chromosomes— some are loving— and some are mixed with strands of hate— but we're mainly dealing with our emotions and our DNA.

Some say that things just happen— some say that they were born that way.

Alternating sides whether it's love or hate— blood is thicker than water— but some family members just don't want to see you be great.

What to do now— do we reciprocate the hate— return it— give back to them their same forms of hate?

Love is a choice— unlike our DNA— we can't control our birth, or family members when they make repeated mistakes.

We can still try to love no matter the complications— but sometimes it just doesn't work. — Some people are better left alone and kept at a distance.

Experiencing a difficult family member can be stressful when you really want to be there for them, but they won't let you.

Sometimes even when you know that they have behavioral issues, or whatever their situation may be. You just can't help them because they may not allow you to express your love, regardless of your genetic connection.

And have you ever had to experience the blood is thicker than water notion, as it pertains to having to choose someone over someone else because of your DNA relation? Or do you not use that notion very often because you know that sometimes your own bloodline is more harmful than anyone else, so you don't have a problem with choosing a loyal friend over family?

Good or bad, what are your thoughts?

'Poetic Wisdom for Life'

Who Are You?

That business person— a professional with a trade that builds and proposes deals— attempting to make a profit.

That scientist person with a brain of strong knowledge dealing with a body of facts— observing and experimenting.

That artist person— sculpturing— producing— and reflecting.

Have you not yet picked your methods of living? Determining characteristics of something essential to your qualities of being.

Originating from where? Only you know, and you can be whatever you want to be. Even if you're just starting your journey today.

Under construction or fully prepared— you are the best, upbeat, mindful, and as headstrong as you need to be.

Capable of everything— filled with substance and intended for good— you're ethical and loved.

Skilled and guided with principles— you're exemplified with great leadership, as you be you and do what you must do.

You are one of God's greatest creations, made with love and in his image.

If you ask yourself, or if someone else ask you who are you besides your name. How would you answer that question?

So many of us have gotten lost at some point in our lives trying to be something or someone whom we are not.

How often do you experience times when you feel lost? Or do you usually know who you are and what you want and how you want it?

Use the space on the next page to talk about your journey of knowing who you are.

And if you're still trying to figure it out, express your thoughts by writing down your plans of how you intend to understand you more.

'Poetic Wisdom for Life'

BRAIN FOOD

We're Better Now

The days were long and the nights longer— fussing and fighting seemed to be more relevant than cuddling.

Opposite directions became evident— with too many oppositions, so we split— no more confusion as the fear to leave each other disappeared.

We're better now— honest— and there's no more hiding secrets. No more questioning loyalty and wishing to be anywhere else but within the presence of our own sheets.

I cheated on you— you cheated on me— no faithfulness— just stuck together for money, kids, and other responsibilities. No matter how much the stress got too deep, we stuck with it and remained unhappy.

Family ties are good when we compromise— and being great leaders is far more important than fighting because things didn't work out.

No one hating is how it works best— and being thankful for other replacements to lean on is wise as we continue to move forward every day.

The satisfaction of not having so many bad distractions is what to strive for— not to be mad, and dig ourselves into a bigger and much deeper hole.

When you're in a committed relationship, it's normal to experience ups and downs because that's just how life goes.
But if you're constantly revisiting unnecessary problems, then maybe a deeper issue is existing that needs to be addressed.

Fixing relationships by compromising can be felt through a spouse, friend, family member, coworker, etc.
Things can become better through compromising versus fighting, but have you ever had to dismiss someone because there was just absolutely no way of working things out as far as you were concerned?

If so, how were you able to move forward without fixing it?
And if you've experienced the satisfaction of compromising and adjusting to make you and whomever else feel better. What was that experience like?

'Poetic Wisdom for Life'

BRAIN FOOD

Today's Date

Wake up— no time to drool— daylight is present— time to get up— start the day whether it's work or school.

How do you live— what's your daily duties— what do you strive for— what's on your agenda?

Widespread or small steps— make your business a walk of success— do it for yourself or for the love of others who are present.

Carry on your name and stamp it without shame— rise above any struggles because struggles are just a key part of your life span.

Invest in yourself and accept help— pass along your wealth while still protecting it and your good health.

Today is a day of actions— even with infractions from love ones and others that causes unnecessary distractions.

Shake it off.

It's all about you and your life— and how you're moving forward— because as of today, you refuse to go backwards.

This title, Today's Date, came about after waking up one day and having to really encourage myself to keep moving forward.
I felt blessed and happy to be alive, so I wrote about carrying my name forward even through my struggles.

How do you carry on your name as you plan your day while staying encouraged to invest in yourself on a day like today?

Use the space below and on the next page to describe your thoughts regarding today's date.

Right now, is it morning, noon, or night?

How are you feeling?

_____
_____

'Poetic Wisdom for Life'

BRAIN FOOD

Love Mate

I long for the embracing of your arms and hearing your whispers through the soft breeze that covers the night.

I unfold myself during the presence of your body— and feel the warmness evoking from your touch.

Your love travels down beneath my pores— I'm happy and excited because I love you so much.

The kisses from your moist lips leaves behind a desire for more— I try to ignore the urge to slide my body against yours.

We'll forever link in peace with the presence of our love encircling us— as I gaze into your beautiful eyes— I'll always feel blessed.

Stronger than spoken words can speak— you ignite me with goose bumps from my head to even beyond my feet— because your love has taken over me.

You lead as we escape into our world of beautiful fantasies— I feel the essence of our bond locking in strong— so I know I must be careful.

I'm inspired but I don't want to get lost— because falling deeper in love can be scary due to the fear of loving you more than I love myself.

But wisdom is here, so I won't forget to love myself— I just need for you to know that you must love yourself also— before you can truly love someone else.

After reading this poem, have you ever experienced similar loving feelings for someone? If so, did your love last or has it now ended?

Some of us love hard, and of course sometimes it works out, and sometimes it doesn't.
Use the space on the next page to write about your situation, talk about if you've ever experienced such a love mate.
Did you care more for that person than you did for yourself mentally, physically, or financially? Or did your love mate turn out to be exactly what you wanted and needed even as of today?

'Poetic Wisdom for Life'

Views

Dance like no one is watching— and teach good stuff even when it isn't popular— love through hate and know that gaining respect is something that no one can take.

Even when you think that no one is watching— be great, because you may get more views in life than you think.

Online or offline, spread your love wisely. — After all, if you don't help show us the right way, our future generations may suffer.

Right now there's lopsided visions of false news— with a bird's eye view of what not to do— it's unevenly balanced but you can help change the news.

Leaning to one side is never a good move— view all sides then make the best decisions that will help me and you.

Knowledge is power— just know that I see you and others do too— give us something positive to watch, because your life is on display for others to view.

Be you.

There's nothing or no one better to choose— God made you like you are— so live authentically and give thanks to him for creating you.

When it comes to views, it's not all about the internet and who sees you. Although it's important to understand why and what you're happily releasing into this world for strangers to view.
But also offline, who has their eyes on you?

How available are you to people? And not just family and friends, but to all people including coworkers and strangers too.

I'm always speaking about privacy and how important it is to be discreet about our personal lives, business lives, and even our general everyday family lives. Because not everyone that smiles in our faces has a positive interest in us. And although people know this already, some of us still tend to want everyone to see us and what we have.
How do you feel about your views?

'Poetic Wisdom for Life'

BRAIN FOOD

Education in Us

General knowledge is acquired first through family— through whom we're connected to because we learn from those around us— even before we're old enough to talk.

Developing the powers of reasoning and judgment— young minds need parents and other good qualified teachers and adults.

Education starts at home— and for those of us who were less fortunate— our process of teaching should guide our future into being different.

Let's educate ourselves as well as talk to our elders— because their words of wisdom is helpful. And can save us from less corruption.

Training in some schools are cool— but stay aware because some communities are suffering— some people feel like they are less important.

Intellect has a big effect— it has power— it facilitates growth.

Talk to the teachers in your community as we all learn more— because our knowledge mixed with their knowledge is more than just important.

The power of education lives within us— our knowledge is power— self-control is strength, right thought is mastery, so be calm and use your power wisely.

I like to surround myself with people who talk about visions and ideas; not people who talk about other people.
So when I talk about personal growth and education, it's because of the essential things in life that helps us.
Versus the non-essential things that oftentimes hurt us.

Some of us are aware enough to know that we have a lot of flaws, but wise enough to know that our heart is pure, and our souls are filled with good vibes while we attempt to help others as we also continue to learn, grow, and help ourselves.

How do you view your education within you?
Do you share your experiences with others, or do you usually keep what you've learned to yourself?

'Poetic Wisdom for Life'

Lost Angel

I thought of all the nights I sank in endless pain— lost in a sick mind and a filthy body of sin.

Thinking I was the ruling spider— but I was stuck in a lethal spider's web— stashed away and ready to be eaten alive.

Staring at a rusty mirror and watching my reflection dissolve— the soul of a lost angel— tampered with and messed up.

Feeling useless and lost— I hurt me then I save me— I should never be a personal haven for anyone to do me wrong, or allow any disrespect upon me.

Every breath taken is hope for more sanity— but like an infant experiencing an open cut for the first time— I'm hurt and need someone to care for me.

Male or female— we all have feelings— we all bleed— even the lost souls needs saving. They need help finding their way.

Some are stuck watching people live great lives— because breaking free to live their own lives is a big challenge that they're afraid of.

But don't fear being free from confinement— you deserve to be free, so power through and succeed— never give up on your freedom.

Sometimes it can be very difficult to pull yourself out of a painful situation, especially if you've been in that situation for a longtime, and you really don't know how to get out of it.
No matter how bad you want to be free, it's like you're a lost angel with no clue of how to get that release.
But for some people, being a prisoner in your own mind can also hold you in such captivity.

Have you ever been, or do you know of anyone whom you feel is a Lost Angel?
We all need help and can use someone that's genuinely willing to help us if we're ever feeling lost. But so many things can have a person feeling like they can't help themselves, and neither can anyone else help them.

What are your thoughts?

'Poetic Wisdom for Life'

BRAIN FOOD

<u>Create Your Way</u>

Lay outside and take in some fresh air— stretch out and spread your limbs— be stress free while thinking about life and what's in it.

Create your path and live this way— it'll last— pass on your knowledge to help others survive.

There's enough turmoil with untrusting people and their evil ways— including violence— it's sad, but it's a common thing.

Rise up and have fun while you create your own way— and hang around leaders that see your worth— as you continue to shine and live in abundance every day.

Getting lost is easy— but finding how to be yourself in a world of uncertainty can be hard and feel unrewarding.

But that's why creating your own way is so important— because you'll form a different way of thinking— and it'll be so real and rewarding.

Have you ever felt misplaced in life, but quickly found yourself creating a better way?

You didn't get stressed out, stretched out, and spread all over the place. You trusted in your abilities and did things your own way. If this has ever been you, how did you manage to get to that place? Or for you, it's still a work in progress type of thing?

Sometimes it helps people when they feel confined, it makes them stop and evaluate things. It makes them take a closer look at themselves and what they want to be, and that makes them change.

But even if you never feel closed in, use the space on the next page to express your thoughts on the highs and lows of creating your own way.

How often do you sit back and take in some fresh air as you think, strategize, and have fun planning and creating?

And what are your thoughts to keep from getting overwhelmed when you're attempting to evolve into creating your own way?

'Poetic Wisdom for Life'

Eye Contact

I'm too nervous to look up because I know that you're watching me— I like you but I'm shy— too bashful to say hi.

Too afraid to look you in your eyes— or even realize what's really in front of me— maybe this is where my future abides.

I won't know unless I let go and see— trust myself while taking things slow and being safe but opened.

Opening-up is the only way to know what's ahead of me— as I look up and pray— asking God for more knowledge as he guides me every day.

Eye contact is important— it connects— it shows strength and not just to you or me. But to whomever you're trying to connect with— some people will even say; look at me when you talk to me.

Say hi— be present— polite— and not too aggressive. Confidence is great— but don't become annoying and causing headaches.

Live— hold your head up and speak— look at people and don't be afraid to say how you feel.

Some people really do feel uncomfortable looking people in their eyes when they're communicating.
They may glance at you a few times, or even briefly look at your eyes, but never full eye contact for very long at any point during the conversation.

And I've heard all types of reasons and opinions about the type of people who can't seem to look a person in their eyes when they're communicating.

Everything from them being not so trustworthy people, to there's nothing wrong with them at all. Eye contact simply makes them uncomfortable, and that's it.

What are your thoughts on how it makes you feel when a person can't keep eye contact with you when you're communicating?

Does it not matter to you about their eye contact, because their words and actions are all that matters to you? What are your thoughts?

'Poetic Wisdom for Life'

<u>Spreading Love</u>

Correct me— tell me I'm wrong— show me the way— reach out to me so that we can experience compromise, things can be your way and mine.

Happy days are ahead with big smiles and giggling— always chuckling through lots of laughter while wearing genuine smiles and grins.

Dancing, cheering, and chanting with so many good vibes appearing— as we release any guilt of our past transgressions.

Smothered in love— kindness— joy and happiness— thanks for correcting me. Our lives are more than just tragedies, hard living and crying. Let's be more like Kings and Queens rising.

Live— laugh— love and let go, be set free of the bad things that hold you down. Don't forget it, but understand that those things are no longer yours.

Really— pray for control— live life as if you already have what you need— even if you don't, because it's coming just hold on. You'll see.

Spread your love and let nature take control— your natural instincts will tell you what to do. Distribute good auras and hopefully others will follow.

Spreading love isn't very hard to do, although these days we must be cautious in everything we do. Including the way we spread our love around to people we don't know.

In your opinion, do you feel that it's okay to naturally spread your love around even to strangers? Or do you feel that it's okay to love people, but at a distance because you prefer to be a bit more cautious with your love? Meaning you're slow to love and hug on people, especially strangers, due to the possibilities of your love being misplaced?

Use the space below and on the next page to talk about your love habits if you have any. And if you call your love expressions something other than love habits, talk about that and your ways of spreading that love.

Love is more common than hate. — Is that statement true or false?

_____
_____

'Poetic Wisdom for Life'

Capable Flower

You're a seed that flourishes— growing beautifully and vigorously thriving, and being prosperous.

You are robust— suited to be rich and filled with great taste— soft— yet stoutly built while producing a gorgeous view.

Wanted by many but only taken care of by a few— attention needed— but you can sprout without it, because you do what you must do.

You bloom— into a beautiful you— one of the finest humans we've ever seen.

Cultivated— refined— and capable of anything— adored by many as you dwell and be around great things.

Elegant— pure— courteous and civilized— you're ready to be a delicate source of comfort at any time.

Like fresh air on a nice summer day— you are just what's needed— a breath of fresh air capable of providing wonderful feelings.

A flower is usually described as the part of a plant that is often brightly colored, and usually lasts a short time. It's cultivated for its floral beauty. But oftentimes the comparison of a flower is loved because of its reproductive structure and ability to flourish.

I use it because it's time for our beauty to flourish like a flower, and I'm a witness that we are capable of flourishing into whatever we want to be with a little care.

Like a flower we can have a healthy appearance indicating freshness and beauty, but this poem is intended to have you look more into that notion to see if you feel like you are indeed robust, strong, and healthy inside and out; so that you can flourish.
Get ready to bloom, and be elegant and capable of comforting others.

Use the space to describe your most recent flourishing moments.

_____
_____

'Poetic Wisdom for Life'

BRAIN FOOD

Sweetness

Taste like fruit— juicy— sweet— but not too much— although it's healthy and recommended by doctors. The taste is good for you, but it can also be bad too.

Too much of anything can be unhealthy— so take your time— don't indulge, go slowly.

What do you like most about any sweetness? How much do you love it? Does it have a hold on you?

Does it control you? Are you addiction prone with your mouth wide open— can you not live without it?

You touch it— accept it— and with sweet sensations of its comfortable presence, you'll never let go because you're afraid you'll lose it forever.

You want to be bold— strong— and not hold on so tightly, but with its grips of love you'll do whatever's next to make the sweetness last longer.

That's unhealthy— it won't keep you happy.

Understand that there's nothing better than a strong sweet presence— but without balance a lot can go wrong.

Give out your sweetness— also receive yours— just always think ahead, because the reality of too much sweetness can do a lot of good and a lot of bad; it's up to you to balance it all out.

Use the space to explain your thoughts. And if you have ever been addicted to any kind of sweetness; food, a person, or whatever.

How did you become addicted, and how did you get better?

Sometimes things happen and some of us allow certain things or people to control us with sweetness, and when the sweetness becomes bitter sweet, it can make us sick.

Have you ever been controlled by any kind of sweetness?
Or is controlled too strong of a word to describe your sweet experience?

'Poetic Wisdom for Life'

Women and Men

A female human being— she's set apart from a girl or a boy— she's a grown lady— plus male, she's a female.

Characterized from a boy or a woman— he's a male person— a man— he's a masculine species— he's tough and asserting.

How do you see yourself— man versus woman— we're all the same but different.

Beautiful spirits with kind hearts— we stay attached even when we're apart.

Although the choices we make can put a dent in our hearts— whether you're a male or female— some of us love hard.

We can love hard and protest hate— we are all strong human beings— especially when we pull together and trust each other with faith.

Let's support one another because we're marvelous when we're joined together— things won't be perfect— all we can do is work at it.

Whether you're a man or a woman— your instincts will guide you through— be independent but still look out for each other too.

What are your thoughts when it comes to women and men?

I've heard people say that women are smarter than men, and vice versa.

But it's also been said that we are all equal to a certain extent.

And I'm usually quiet and very observant when people are discussing women and men and our similarities, along with their thoughts and opinions regarding men versus women.
I just sit and listen.

But as you've read above, through it all, I feel like regardless of what's happening. — We're a force when we're all together.

Do you feel the same way, or do you honestly feel like one is more superior over the other?

'Poetic Wisdom for Life'

Autism and being Unique

Judged by certain challenges— with unique strengths and differences— autism speaks, but do we listen?

What condition urges you to pay attention? And with a widespread spectrum of extensions— it's good because our world could use more brilliant visions.

A combination of different forms— some people need a variation of attention.

Support from others will development more influences— and allow more visions to come through and offer their attention.

Everyone is different— but with some control we can all see our strengths— and even our same capabilities regardless of our appearances.

We are all human and have our own gifts— so being strictly identified by how we were born may not always be best, so let's get to know people first.

Speak to me— be unique— even if you hear or see a disability— remember that's only a small part of us human beings.

We all have our own delays— but communication helps us all.
Let's not judge each other without knowing anything about the others flaws.

Hearing different stories about autism is interesting because oftentimes no matter how the conversation goes, I see familiarities.

Have you ever been around anyone with autism? Or even more than that, are you the parent of an autistic child?

If you can identify with anything referring to autism and being unique, explain your experiences.

And if you haven't been around anyone with autism, or any other condition that's different from whatever you may be used to.

Whatever it may be, if you don't know much about it, that's okay. Do some research and get more familiar with it as of today. We're all better when we're educated.

'Poetic Wisdom for Life'

<u>*Dance with Me*</u>

Let's dance— prance around like we're on top of the world— enjoying livelihood while living good with trust and faith.

Clap your hands and move your feet— wave your arms around and join in this dance with me.

Will you have a good day today— it's up to you— therefore I suggest smiling and not letting anyone mess up your dancing good mood.

Do your dance and paint the scenes with love— override any obscenities while jumping around like a toddler filled with sugar and the sweetness of fun times mixed with love and joy.

Let's capture our connections with compelling passion— affection— and positive influences. — Today we'll dance around and fill every room with happiness.

Move your body and let's have some fun— I feel like even at this moment we're expressing ourselves and releasing love arrows.

And we do this with warm attachments of love and hope— and it doesn't matter our race or our financial status; bonding is our glue.

We're all living organisms— composed of mutual reliance— but can we all really dance around with no bias, and truly be satisfied and happy with life?

Is there anyone in your life that makes you feel like dancing around all day and truly paint the scenes with love no matter where you go?

How mutual are we to form a reliance of trust?
How likely are we to accept our differences and live without bias no matter our race, gender, or financial status?

Strive to feel positive and take in as much love as you can take.
So if you feel like dancing around like you're filled with sugar, or if you truly just feel like being happy all day. — Do that.

You have a right to spread that kind of love around, especially since this world already has enough hate.

'Poetic Wisdom for Life'

BRAIN FOOD

<u>100 Percent</u>

Go big or go home is what some of us say as we strive to be grand in every way— doing our best is what makes us more and never less.

How we feel about ourselves can be seen by others even before we speak— so represent you properly.

Your presence is massive— you're a blessing to this earth intended for good.

100% is what to give— even if it's only baby steps in the right direction— those small steps of our best efforts will guide us into more greatness.

Giving it our all is always winning— especially when our one hundred percent means that we're living our lives at our own individual paces.

Our own percentage for life is always greater— and that's why jeopardizing our own spirits for any other lifestyles than our own is not our best living.

Spiritual growth leads to more mental growth and so much more— let's enjoy our lives and our lifestyles as we grow.

Spreading our joy with our percentages of more— is a recipe for happy times and fun memories filled with laughter and hope.

And for anyone living fifty percent or lower— if it's positive keep living and doing your best, you'll get what you need as you keep growing.

I'll be the first to admit that I'm not always operating at 100% every day, but even under 100%, I do my best while knowing that I'm not perfect.

How do you handle yourself when you feel like you're not at your best?

Some days our mental, physical, emotional, and especially our financial responsibilities can be strained and cause us not to feel good.

But the win comes when we do as best as we can even at 10%, because if we keep going while avoiding unnecessary distractions. We can all reach a great amount of our full potential.

What are your thoughts?

'Poetic Wisdom for Life'

Score

We win some and we lose some— who's our competitors— our rivals— can our opponents block us?

Are they scoring? Are they frustrating us, making us emotional with a consciousness of strong feelings that can destroy us?

The answer is no. Because we increase, if they score then we score. And there are no other possibilities— because our only mission is winning.

When playing this game of life— it's like a puzzle of mysteries— a game of unforeseen experiences mixed with reactions of others who are also living.

Playing your part is a dramatic composition composed and managed by you— the growing elements of life makes us all want more.

Getting in formation to score and resist anything that tries to come against us is how to achieve this win and become whole.

Let's focus on our life goals as we organize and get structured to achieve more.

The process may not always be easy— but it's worth our time and effort to win in life as we spread our scoring techniques.

Protect your health and your wealth— while remembering that if scoring ever becomes easy for you— it's okay to still perform as if you've never won anything before.

How often do you focus on your winning goals?

How do you score? And would you like to see a replay?
Are your current ways of living helping you to win and properly managed things? What does that look like, how do you accomplish winning?

Exercising our rights is a serious performance activity.
How do you exercise your rights? How do you set yourself up to win and become a champion in your own life of scoring?

Are you disappointed or happy with your score card right now?

'Poetic Wisdom for Life'

The End

Is it ever over— because the end could be the beginning— life is what you make of it, so live your life without regrets.

Trust the process because sometimes greatness comes with many tests.

Work hard— live— and even during struggles and disappointments, forgive and show strength.

You were made special— extraordinary and very important— therefore, never forget the one who gives you the test is also the one who gives you the answers.

Seek God because every life needs covering— every life needs protection— and don't pray in faith and live in doubt, believe in your prayers and make things happen.

We all need guidance so follow your heart and do what you feel is right— just remember that praying and planning goes together.

Don't sit around doing nothing and expect things to happen— trust the Lord and yourself as you earn your way.

Use God's resources to help push you forward— while staying aware and never giving up.

Use the spaces on the next few pages to express whatever you want to express, because there is no ending to our uplifting and being here for each other.

You can write a poem, or think about your wisdom overall, then pen it.

You can even start from the beginning of this book and read your entries, then come back and write down your overall experience.

Whatever you choose to do at this point is up to you, but hopefully this book has helped you like it's helped me.
My brain is still eating!

Thank you for reading and participating!

'Poetic Wisdom for Life'

BRAIN FOOD

'Poetic Wisdom for Life'

I would love to hear your thoughts and views about life as you know it, so please reach out via website or any of my social media platforms!

Live. Laugh. Love.

Those are three common words used to motivate and inspire, just as the common saying. "I never lose— I either win or I learn".

And since I agree with it all, these words are just reminders to continue to stay motivated and to acknowledge *your* strengths as *you* let it guide *you* into *your* future.

Even during hard times surrounded by dead end paths, remember to go instead where there is no path, and leave a trail.

Acknowledging that honesty is the first chapter in the book of wisdom is a wise choice, so be knowledgeable and honest with yourself and everything else will eventually fall into its rightful place.

Nonetheless, some of the best advice that I've received, and will continue to pass along is that thinking for yourself and having discipline is the bridge between goals and accomplishments.

Be strong and never give up on yourself. And support others as you would want them to support you.

We are under no obligations to be the same person that we were a year, a month, or even 15 minutes ago.

No matter what's happening in your life, be sure to take pride in supporting and promoting positivity and peace. Because our lives becomes a masterpiece when we learn how to master peace.

Therefore, how you perceive life is how you will receive life; it's your choice.

In order to love who you are, you cannot hate the experiences that shaped you, so love you and what made you.

'Poetic Wisdom for Life'

Be Great!

ABOUT THE AUTHOR

Meko is passionate about her journey in writing, and as she continues to pen her poetry every day, she remains dedicated to helping others to do the same.

Brain Food has been a vision of hers to provide readers a way to reflect and gather more ways for a positive life.

Grateful and excited to present this book aiming to help others, she is currently working on more self-help books, nonfiction books, fiction novels, and so much more.

Share your experiences with other readers and with Meko as she continues to entertain, uplift, and encourage growth.

For more of her books, and for more general information about Meko and Eagle Life. Visit www.eaglelifepublications.net.

Let's Connect!

'Poetic Wisdom for Life'

Made in the USA
Middletown, DE
15 November 2024

64625294R00104